These Five Words Are Mine

Conversations With Life. My Journey to
Awareness... Five Words at a Time.

Jennifer Lynne Croneberger

authorHOUSE®

AuthorHouse™
1663 Liberty Drive
Bloomington, IN 47403
www.authorhouse.com
Phone: 1-800-839-8640

Published by AuthorHouse 12/10/2012

ISBN: 978-1-4772-9681-3 (sc)
ISBN: 978-1-4772-9680-6 (hc)
ISBN: 978-1-4772-9684-4 (e)

Library of Congress Control Number: 2012922991

Photo credit: Mauricio Merlo. Cover Design: Tim Croneberger

This book is printed on acid-free paper.

Contents

Part One.

Part Two.

Part Three.

Part Four.

Part Five.

Foreword

When we spend most of our days "getting through" them, "getting by" or "surviving," we are missing the magic in life. This is no secret. Those of us who have seen the magic know this to be true.

But even those of us who have seen it - can still get caught up in the *day to day.* <u>We forget to look.</u> We forget to truly open our eyes and pay close attention to all that is.

We take for granted the little things. We live in moments where some are outstanding, others are not so much, but we rarely look at the collective and just how grand the magnitude is of that collective.

That's exactly what Jen Croneberger does in this book. She shares her own collection of moments – and takes us with her through them, while subtly, but powerfully, showing us the magic as well.

She shows us *just how beautiful life really is*. Even through some of the toughest or most emotionally wrought moments – there is beauty. And if we never really thought there could be, this book is the ONLY PROOF one needs that we were wrong. Dead wrong.

I myself and many I know have always been positive and/or optimistic. This book isn't at all about that, though it certainly expresses the power of said mind-set.

This book is about the glimmers of hope, the silver linings, the unseen – if unaware.

The lessons we learn from this book are subtle but incredibly beautiful. They are life lessons we all need to learn. Many of us do so on our own time, in our own ways but this book shows us a faster way -- A way for today, tomorrow and every day going forward.

When you learn to look through Jen's eyes – *{the eyes of someone who just appreciates life, is present in every moment, lives with heart, understands the value of grace and the power of not settling for less than you deserve}* **you see the world differently**. You might even see the book differently. Maybe all books as well. Rereading it will prove that too (as I have done so twice now myself).

And while I am not yet known to you, I hope that my perspective on Jen's story is one you will share.

Yes, we are distant through geography but as close and connected as any humans ever have been with technology. We see new possibilities and start to realize that if we can dream it – it can happen. Our collective consciousness is changing with us too. How can it not? Through technology the distances between us are closing. The connectedness we can have is limitless. We know now that "seeing" others and recognizing that everyone plays a different part in our stories – whether we know WHY or not – makes a difference now. We know it because we can see it now. We can hear it and feel it. We are awake. Or at least we can be if we open our eyes to see the kind of magic we are talking about here.

The truth is, all through life our perspectives have been altered by the things we see, hear or do. We are, after all, a makeup of all of that. Sometimes even without knowledge.

When we *open our eyes though* and acknowledge that this magic is unfolding in all of those moments -- we cannot deny the grandeur of it all.

Jen clearly illustrates in this book. She shows how looking back – we see things we never saw at the time. Looking back with new perspective breathes more life into life itself.

I know that every day when a client approaches me about a feeling of disconnect they have in their businesses – all it takes is a "look back" at where they started, why they were there, what they (or their markets) have gone through and how change along the way may have taken them off track. In some cases they want to get back to where they started again and in other cases they want to rewrite the plan. Many will realize things they never noticed about themselves or their businesses when doing this as well. Some will complain, while others stand in shock and disbelief that little miracles have been lying there waiting to be recognized for far longer than they needed to be.

But one thing is always clear. If we don't look back, <u>eventually we get in our own way</u>. How we choose to deal with that makes all the difference.

So instead of staying busy, living day by day, moment to moment or just getting by – why not take time out to look back? Isn't that where the magic lives anyhow? I know you want to see it too.

Having been through this numerous times myself I can say that looking back does reveal the magic. Not necessarily because the magic was always there but because it allows us to reflect, accept, change our perspective on the story, change our future and usher in new magic; magic we see in the here and now – not just yesterday.

Jen Croneberger's stories not only prove this is possible but she lights the fire under us to ensure that it is. This book is yet another remarkable read from a fellow Free Thinking Renegade and to say that it is inspiring is an understatement. **It's mind bending – that's what it is.**

Throughout most of "The Five Words", I found myself stepping back to reflect on my own life and acknowledge my own perspectives and how they have changed over the years. I saw more magic and created more as well. It is without a doubt a game changer.

When you read it, I am sure you too will see that **"It *really* is beautiful in here"**!

Cijaye DePradine – The RePurposing Coach. Author of "Re-Inventing For A Purpose". CijayeDePradine.com

Preface

When I was in second grade, I wrote my first book. And another in third and one in fourth. We wrote books all the time. It was my favorite part of school.

I wrote my first poem when I was seven. I have always been a writer in my mind. But one of my lifelong goals since I was that young was to write a book… and have it published. The ability to hold the book in my hands was something I have honestly woken up, dreaming about.

For years, I have told myself stories; why I couldn't do that or why no one would want to read it… or even that I wasn't good enough. Who am I really? To throw the word author next to my name is something I have longed for. Not for a feeling of status, but for the feeling of a self-fulfilled goal. For realizing who I really am. For rewriting the story I have long told myself. Changing the 'can't" to "can"… and finally taking the action to make it happen.

Through the following chapters you will read a collection of stories. Stories from my life that I've shared with others and now you. Stories that "together" make a difference in my own life and remind me that there is always something greater at work. I believe these stories prove that sometimes we take things a little too seriously or think too much about something all while missing the real magic life has to offer. This collection of stories is the magic I want to share with you. From my heart to yours, I hope you start to see the magic in your own life too.

Dedication

To Mom and Dad, the heroes who left footprints on my heart and in my soul forever. You taught me who and what I am. And gave me more than a child should ever need. Your support and unwavering faith in me have made me who and what I am today.

You believed in me when I didn't. Thank you isn't nearly enough.
You certainly have given me both roots and wings.
You are the inspiration for my drive and my reminder of how powerful the support of family can be.
My wings definitely work. And yes, my roots are strong.
Thank you for your unconditional love... I couldn't be all of this without you.

To my sisters and brother, you always supported me and were often times my biggest fans. You taught me real love. I am blessed to be a part of a family with such real bonds. I love each of you deeply. Thank you for all you are and what you give to me. Nothing is as strong as the love of family.

To my friends, coaches and teachers who have inspired me along my journey...
You have played a role in my life in countless ways.

Thank you for making me always feel like I can take on the world.

This is just the beginning. Allow me to pay you back... I promise to be a student always.

I am most certainly complete. Thank you for showing me love and understanding, patience and surrender. Thank you for inspiring me to be all that I am. I am a better person because of you... This was truly a labor of love. Here it is, finally... my book. To you: my forever gratitude.

To Mauricio Merlo for the photography on the covers, to Tim Croneberger for the cover design, to Cijaye DePradine for the foreword that adds such wisdom to this book, to Ed White for the thorough editing of the manuscript. To the countless friends who read and gave feedback. Thank you for contributing to this endeavor. I wouldn't have been able to make this happen without each of you.

I leave you to enjoy my thoughts and experiences along my journey. This book is a collection of some of my favorite blogs as well as a story that unfolded in a simple way around the lessons life has taught me. Together, it tells a story of awareness. It is amazing to me what the world looks like when you open your eyes for the first time. I am here, present with you.

Here's to seeing life with new eyes.

Agape,

Jen

Introduction

She flipped her sunglasses onto her head as a mere suggestion.
It was hot - and brighter than yesterday.
But she always felt it rude not to speak eye to eye.

He looked away, almost to brush off the gesture with a passive-aggressive air.

"Are you going to talk to me?"
There was a chill in the sultry 96-degree air. He was clearly avoiding her. And it was starting to piss her off.

"Hey… Can you hear me? Why are you ignoring me?"

He turned to look at her slowly, her own eyes reflecting off of his mirrored aviators.

"What?" He was abrupt, cool, and without feeling.

She moved closer, the sun radiating off of her shoulders as if it didn't belong there. The rays bounced to his face.

"I asked you a question…" She sat still, not moving an inch, in hopes that he would feel the warmth on his face and give in to her.

"I didn't hear you... And I'm sure you will ask again."

She was feeling the warmth rise to her left ear. Her pulse quickened. She was tired of this game.

How many times would she ask him something and he would just ignore her?

How many times would he give her answers that made no sense, or were empty and without help?

She was growing disenchanted with the continued back and forth.

Just as she was about to get up, he responded.

He lifted up his shades...

"You already have all the answers you will ever need. I told you that last Thursday. And the Sunday before.

When will you listen?"

Part One.

Awareness

"The truth is, I know myself deeper than I let on. I have a choice to see things for what they are or fool myself with empty wishes and washed up dreams. I will find a true sense of belonging in these pages. For when I feel lost the most... I am really being found." --jlc

"Do you have a plan?" he asked with an annoyance in his voice, his tone booming in an echo much like the thunderstorm the night before. She looked up sheepishly from her book just slowly enough not to make her head pound any more than it already was. Her heart was racing. Her palms were sweaty . Just like the day before... and the day before that one. And sometime last June when he asked in the same tone.

"A plan?" she muttered back. "What kind of plan are you talking about?" The disgruntled shakiness in her voice made it clear she didn't even like the question, let alone the need to answer it. Her nerves were like butterflies being released from the net for the first time in their lives.

"He will laugh at me," she thought to herself. "Who doesn't make a plan? I mean, I certainly don't have one, but obviously...I should."

As she got up to leave, she figured her departure would just end the conversation anyway and she wouldn't have to reply to his awkward question.

She felt a gentle hold on her forearm, the fingers clenching her tighter with each second she didn't move. And just then, she realized that her awareness of something bigger became her plan of sorts. It was enough. It was exactly what she needed and longed for.

Life didn't provide a plan for her... Or at least it didn't really show itself when she needed it most. He laughed, just as she suspected. And then his grip tightened.

Life is like that. It holds on. It lets go. And she worried too much about what she couldn't control. She awoke from a long sleep wondering if it would ever change. Awake ... with her eyes shut... Still.

The way he laughed... it stuck with her. She felt like maybe she needed to have it all laid out. That maybe, since she was such a perfectionist, it would never be good enough. She would never be satisfied with what is? ... and always wondered "what if?"

And as life's grip closed around her bones, she closed tighter, too. And it made for a choking heaviness that wouldn't let her sleep at night.

And then... one bright sunny fall day in late October, he let go. Or at least loosened his grip. She was aware of her pulse slowing down, of her ability to breathe more regularly. Of feeling a freedom she never knew. She felt more alive. He loosened the grip some more.

"So this is awareness," she thought to herself. And all of a sudden the picture was colorful.

She laughed, not to mock him, but to remind herself of that sound.

She got up to walk away and found herself going nowhere.

She was finally home.

He laughed as he stood to leave.

"Stay," she said convincingly. "I am ready."

Chapter 1

Heart separates us from others

The Latin word for heart is "cor." The word courage originally meant to be able to tell the story of who you are with your whole heart, and with feeling. We each have a story. From where we were born and grew up to what led us to where we are today. Everyone we pass on the street, too, has a story. We may just never know what it is.

So I realize now that it's not what we look like, it's not what we do for a living or the color of our skin... but our ability to tell the story of who we are, openly, with nothing to hold back, that separates us from each other. It's our story. It's our heart.

I talk to a lot of people in my travels; some are naturally more talkative than others. Some are guarded and quiet. People tell me I am easy to talk to. They ask me what I do to make it easy. I always say I don't know... I just invite others to talk to me I guess. But I get it now... My first job in my profession is to build trust. As I do that, I realize that most of the time, I share my own story with my clients. I relate in any way that I can to show my human side, too. I share my heart.

One of the stories I use often in my work with teams is a personal story of striking out looking at a called third strike in a big softball game. Being human is the easiest way to build trust. I have failed, I have fallen, I have been hurt, and I have hurt others. But one thing will always remain true: My heart tells my story. I know anyone can relate to that.

I was in the nursing home on Christmas visiting with my Mom. I always take time to watch, to listen to and to share some conversation with a few of the regular talkers, those who clearly just like to be heard. There is one gentleman in particular whom I often see. His name is Stewart. He is quiet. He doesn't say much. But this night, he seemed to gravitate toward our table.

We were feeding Mom her supper and visiting with Dad. Stewart wheeled himself over to me and looked at me. With a stern face, he said nothing. He just looked. We laughed and continued on… telling mom silly jokes or something corny my dad undoubtedly said. He was right next to me all of a sudden as I looked over. He said quietly, looking at me sternly, "It's not funny." I was caught off guard for a moment and then turned back to him. I smiled politely and just quietly replied "Awww, yeah it is. If we can't laugh, what good are we?" I looked back at my mom and continued to feed her the chicken corn soup left in her bowl. The dining room was clearing out. The caretakers were putting the food trays away and, one by one, wheeling the residents to their rooms for the night. We carried on. Laughing and talking about the impending snow, then laughing some more.

I saw one of the younger men on his way to bed stuck at the door, the wheels of his chair hooked onto another chair, and he couldn't get unstuck. I got up quickly to go help him out the door. He thanked me after he was done with his little outburst… "Cracker, cracker, cracker," he said in frustration. We managed to get him pointed in the right direction. Just then, walking back to my mom's table, Stewart was in my path. He looked at me with his arms folded. He leaned over and in a quiet, dry, husky voice… like one that has not been used in quite some time, he said, "Do you think it will get better? Because it may not change, you know. Does it get better? In here?" I looked closely, wondering what he meant by this. I saw his hand pointing toward his chest. I questioned quickly, did he mean in HERE? Like, the nursing home? In here, meaning the room where they eat? I mean, I hear the food isn't THAT bad, but maybe not to his liking... or was he really pointing to his heart...? In here, meaning inside? SO many questions, all in a matter of a second. I answered quietly. "Yes, Stewart, it gets better." Not really sure what I was answering, but thinking it was the best option. He wheeled away as I wished him a Merry Christmas, and for the first time, I saw a smile peek through his sternness as he rode off to bed.

I think about that a lot. My sisters and I have talked about it, too. All of the people in that place... they all have a story. They all have heart. They live it every day. Some were doctors, some were teachers and business owners, and homemakers, and counselors. They all have a story.

We often talk about athletes having heart. We say those who play hard have it and those who loaf... well, I guess they don't. But the truth of the matter is, everyone has heart. It is those who have the courage to show it and to live it fully in the face of others whom we celebrate. I have watched athletes give all they have but still come up short. Yet I have seen these same athletes not be afraid to share their story with the world. Courage of champions or something like that... Heart is a choice. It always is.

I have met a lot of Stewarts in my life... Quiet people who don't say much, but when it's time, they remind us of their story. I think I have been Stewart on occasion. At times, I don't think I have the right things to say or the right questions to ask.

"Does it get better?"

I venture to say it does. We have a choice in that.

And I choose to let my heart lead the way. I choose to let my heart tell my story.

My heart will always separate me from others. As will yours.

As will Stewart's.

Chapter 2

If I only had thirty...

If I only had 30 years, I would plan. I would make my time mean something. I would give more, do more, be more. I would make sure that those closest to me know. Not just anything and everything... But know the real stuff - what makes flowers grow toward the sun, why shoelaces are important, why love is what matters most. Really.

I would be careful of who I spent my energy with, where I gave my time. What I did with my extra dessert when I was too full to eat it. Who I would call when I had the best or worst news to share on a simple Thursday at 1:19 p.m. I would rest better once I knew how to spend those 30 years.

If I only had 30 dollars, I would make sure I didn't waste it, I would find the place or person who needed it most. I would give it away, making sure that those who had nothing could at least have something. I wouldn't worry about it, over think it, or second-guess myself. I would give it away without blinking an eye. I would know there was someone else who needed it more. I would rest easier once I knew how to spend those 30 dollars.

If I only had 30 words, I would carefully construct sentences, making sure each word wasn't a waste. I would take out the extras and put in the ones that really mean something. I would spell them all right, taking my time to make sure they were the prettiest of all words - the ones that say the most. I would rest easier once I knew how to write those 30 words.

If I only had 30 miles, I would travel them carefully. No added turns or stops. I would drive slowly, watching for the beauty that surrounds me, even on the paths I have driven a thousand times before. I would see things I ignored or passed quickly, caught up in the rush of everyday life. I would enjoy the feeling of the sun beating down and the wind blowing my hair through the sunroof. I would see every sign, every color, every car, and every animal and person in my sights. I would take my time. I would rest easier once I knew how to drive those 30 miles.

If I only had 30 days, I would spend them with the people I love. I would meet new people I could learn to love and ask those whom I have hurt in any way to forgive me and love me anyway. And in return, I would do the same. I would take longer pauses during conversations to really listen. I would breathe longer and deeper each time I closed my eyes. I would feel grateful for those who have touched my life in so many ways. I would rest easier once I knew how to give back for those 30 days.

If I only had 30 minutes, I would love more and worry less. I would listen more and talk less. I would give more and take less. I would rest easier once I knew how to live those 30 minutes.

If I only had 30 seconds, I would be totally quiet and let my eyes speak without words. I would allow my heart to say what I haven't been able to for 38 years.

Tonight, I will rest easier knowing exactly what I need to do...

...Because waiting for a deadline is what we do when we are waiting to live.

If I only knew...

Chapter 3

I never asked for this...

Yeah. Me neither.

I thought that things only happen when you ask for them. I mean, that's how life works, right? I was sadly mistaken. Life just... happens. No questions asked sometimes. The flat tire, the speeding ticket, the horrible headache and burnt dinner all in one two hour period... people don't really ask for that, right?

I spent some of my evening reading. A funny newfound freedom I feel without classes hanging over me, four chapters of a text and countless articles to digest. I feel good. I can feel again. I was reading some deep stuff, reflecting on life, on mistakes I have made, losses I have accumulated, times I have been so low down. The truth is, we all relate on some level to weakness. We don't often want to admit it, but we relate to it, quietly, suffering in our own cesspool of emotion until maybe someday someone opens the dam and we can lose it all. There is no glory in the junk. By definition, it is just that... Junk. Old broken lamps that don't have a plug, a bulb, or even a switch. What is the point? Buy a new one.

There is some strange kind of a beauty in deep emotion. Even when it is raw and real, there is a softer, more loving conversation we have with ourselves when life gets ugly. It's not my fault. I never asked for this. What else is going to happen? And while this is true, this is the reality of what we have to deal with at any given time. And navigating through the broken lamps often takes careful consideration so as not to cut oneself on the shards of brokenness.

And then that one person comes along with a reminder, like the person who stands a chance at maybe fixing the lamp. The one who picks up the pieces and at least gives it a shot. Because Lord knows you are too afraid to try it yourself. And still, you are left holding the wire, saying... I never asked for this. Maybe you just don't want the help. Maybe not now. Maybe not ever.

Your struggles remain silent, you shuffle through life with sunglasses and a hat on so as not to be seen. You go to work, you come home, you sit on the couch and you go to bed. You get up the next morning, you go to work, you come home, you sit on the couch, and you go to bed. You do it over and over until it becomes a habit, a mindless habit that tears away at your heart muscle, weakening the very fibers it once was. It beats. But not to the same music it once did. It lives in your chest, but you question at times whether it's really yours. And drifting to sleep on a Friday night, you whisper softly... I never asked for this.

And then the day came when you decided you had enough. You wake up and drink orange juice instead of coffee. You drive a different way to work. You say hi to the first person you see, and you smile. Oh, that smile. You missed those muscles working in tandem to create a choice --a word with no voice. Your smile becomes you. Your words pound through your chest. You feel it again. And it feels good. You wonder where it came from... You think life is funny and you go about your day.

Your choice becomes your truth. And little did you know, you never asked for this... any of it.

But congratulations, proud owner...

It's all yours.

Chapter 4

I want to be understood.

There is something pulling on my heart today. It's big. Really big. It's pulling hard…

I spent years wondering why I was here, feeling like I was lost in some kind of emotional tunnel. It was dark. Deep. There was NO … WAY … OUT.

The pulling on me was no match for my pushing against it.

Success eluded me. It was always… just… right… there. And then… poof, it would pull a Houdini and vanish on me. Sometimes, I wouldn't know when to expect it again. Other times, I sat and watched for it… waiting. Quietly. Like a mirage in the desert, always thinking I saw it or knew where it was. Figuring if I was quiet and still, perhaps I wouldn't scare it away this time. I couldn't really define it, this success I was seeking. It kept slipping out of my hands like a balloon string on a windy day.

I wasn't sure of what I wanted. That was clearly the biggest issue.

I was cloudy.

I wanted SOMETHING, but I didn't know what.

I desired SOMETHING, but I felt empty.

It pulled. I pushed.

We didn't get along.

Then came the accolades and awards, all the stuff success was built upon in so many people's mind: the applause, the "can I get my picture with you?" or "Coach Jen, will you sign my ball?"

"Who are you asking?" I thought, almost out loud.

ME? ...WHY ME? I didn't get it... At all. I was trapped in this feeling of success being about what others thought of me.

I was living a daily horror story of a life I didn't really want and one I figured just wouldn't end well.

If I could count how many times I said these words... "I have worked so hard... When will my chance come? When will I finally get a break??" ...It would be in the hundreds. I often wondered why I was destined to feel like I didn't belong anywhere, why I worked hard and felt like I wasn't getting any traction.

Autographs and pictures and applause don't fulfill me. They never will.

I needed more. I wanted more. I desired more. There must be something MORE.

It wasn't fame and fortune that could all be mine that drove me. It still isn't. I think success is in the soul. It's in the connection I felt with others. The eyes that look deeply into mine and respond simply... "I just want to be understood." Yes, I often thought... "Me too."

And maybe as much by myself as by those who look into my eyes and see the guidance they tell me they feel.

My heart has felt full. It has also been emptied in ways I struggle with understanding.

It has ached and yearned and called out for more.

It has recognized that I am more than I have allowed myself to be, or sometimes felt I was capable of, or even deserved.

My heart has led me... often times correctly, sometimes haphazardly, but in any case, it has led me willingly, never boastfully or needing praise.

It has always been my one true guide.

All of a sudden, I had a need to stay true to my heart. Regardless of anything else, I was to follow it. Right, wrong or indifferent, my real understanding was that if I followed my heart it would never be wrong.

My head overthinks and pushes.

My heart corrects it by feeling the pull.

I pushed; it pulled.

Some days, it was an exhausting fight trying to do both at the same time.

I found that doesn't work too well.

Pieces of me would break off, like splinters in the old rail out back.

They hurt when you get too close. The harder you squeeze, the more the splinter drives in, the pain a physical reminder of the fight that continues inside.

So what of this success? Can I call it by name? Whose battle does it become?

My inner warrior was continuing to push. To try to MAKE things happen.

I have to know when to let go of that push and allow the pull to take over. My measure of success is no longer in my head. It's not a fairytale or a movie plot or a story that has a happy ending. In fact, part of the beauty is that I won't know the ending until it comes. That day, one that I hope is far away, will be the day I can answer the question.

Why am I here? Simply to push and pull?

To let go and allow the magic to unfold?

To find ways to create what I desire, not by pushing, but by allowing?

The only push I want to feel is the consistent drive and desire that comes from within. It is not one mandated by thought.

It is formed by the inner gratitude I have found when all else has failed me.

I have pushed. It has pulled.

From now on, I will only ever push on the ocean.

The strong, powerful, vast ocean.

The possibilities of a world surrounding my gentle hand.

The embrace of something so much larger than me.

There, I will feel the tide pull me out to sea.

Set adrift in the ebb and flow of life.

And yes, seeking to understand perhaps maybe more than I seek to be understood.

The water is strong.

It pushes and pulls me in.

My raft is stronger.

I allow it to take me where it will.

I understand now.

I am understood.

"So you want to change the world... Big deal."

He almost laughed out loud at her desire to do big things, his voice demeaning. Patronizing her again because strangely, he felt it was his job to protect her.

She sat staring out at the beauty of the cherry blossoms that popped overnight. The windowpane seemed like a frame that held it, a picture of something not real.

She was ignoring him. Not so much on purpose, but because she just didn't feel like answering him.

"You do know that you can't possibly change the world, right? Like... that's really childish to think..."

He got closer, knowing she wasn't paying attention to anything he said.

Just as he reached out to get her attention, she turned and looked into his eyes.

He felt for a second like she was about to lash out at him.

He took a step back just in case.

"I know."

Simple, to the point.

She didn't want to say another word. She wanted to appease him so he'd just leave.

"Just go away. I'm not going to argue with you today. I'm tired.

I feel beaten." She slumped her head and shoulders like a marionette that a puppeteer had just let fall to the floor.

"Are you happy now?"

He felt heavy.

But with a smirk, he made his way down the yard to rest at the base of the trunk. There, he sat under the cherry blossom tree for a minute to get his bearings.

She stared at its flowers through her windowpane frame for another three and a half hours.

Quiet

And alone.

Chapter 5

Be Audacious. Change the World.

I took a chance once. Who's to say if it was worth it? Chances are, my deep emotions picked it apart. And perhaps I never really knew the answer... or if there was supposed to be one at all... anyway. I always knew I was different. Take that as you will, but I never really fit the mold of those around me. My friends often wanted to contain me in their own pretty little boxes. I was embarrassing them, they would mutter under their breath. Don't get me wrong, I was too self-conscious most often to be that wild and crazy, but I pushed my limits in moments I felt I could. I made people laugh more often than not, all the while cringing inside as my funny faded away.

For some reason, I have often felt alone. In the depths of myself, I have felt like I was missing something. Maybe in my rush to fix things and people, I have neglected the true center of my world... Me. I, too, have often tried to put me in a pretty little box. So I could fit next to the other pretty little boxes in my life. It's a lot neater that way. This is not in any way a plea for a circle of people to make me feel my own worth. I just want to really be authentic with what this means to me. I will try to let my words find their way through the often-misdirected emotions and assumptions.

I have had plenty of friends - close ones, deep ones, friends who knew when to smack me upside the head, and those who let me just be me. I have known there were some who just don't get me. That has always been ok. There are days I just don't get me either. To say we all understand ourselves with never a question would be a rarity. And that, too, is always ok.

I believe it is in the learning process that we truly become what our definition of ourselves is. That changes, yes. But we define it in ways sometimes we don't understand either. And yes... that also is ok. That definition often becomes skewed when we rely on others to validate it. In fact, how can it not? It is OUR definition first and last, and to allow others the power to create words around our very soul just seems... well, wrong.

Why can I say that? I have done it. Often, before I knew better, before I was older and wiser, hell, just yesterday. I found my way back to the center of my world. I wasn't drifting for long... I renegotiated with my WHY. I fought it at times, but I won. This time. The only time that counts.

I have a tattoo around the Apollo Butterfly on my left arm... the words read: "Be the Change." It comes from one of my favorite Gandhi quotes, "Be the change you wish to see in the world." I thought for a long time that meant that I should be the things that I feel are right, and ethical and true, the things I expect to see in others. While that may be true, I found myself wondering more about what the "world" is that I am looking to change. The globe seems pretty big. And we all know the only way to eat an elephant is one bite at a time.

So I picked up the trunk first... Ok, maybe not the visual I am going for here, but I took my first bite. I wanted to give to others. Not the first time, and certainly not a hard thing to do. I created a food drive to help fill the shelves at the Coatesville

Community Food Co-op. Gloria saved my number in her phone. I just may be on speed-dial now. I brought truckloads of food to her warehouse and I still have food to deliver. I found that audacity isn't really that hard when you declare and proclaim what you are going to do. So I did. That's one little world that I helped create change in.

As I look around me to find what else I wish to see change in, I couldn't help but walk past my mirror with my eyes fixated on something else. I dodge my glances. I think maybe there are others who need help. I pick up the phone instead. There is a friend who needs to talk. I take care of some work. I have a feeling my dogs need to go outside. And then I see it... the eyes that look back from the glass as I shut the cabinet door. I am fixated for a minute. I am lost. And for the first time in a while, I see something I haven't seen. I am allowing those eyes to speak, to let go of the things they have held so dear.

I walked to my laptop and began to type. My audacity today has allowed me to be quiet. I wasn't really talkative all day. Barely saying anything to anyone. And that, in this moment, seems ok, too. I realize the silence is my process. I am changing. With that comes a cathartic experience I can't really put into words. You can ask those eyes I saw in the mirror... that center of my world. Me. I don't choose to stay in this moment. Through the deepest pain and the deepest joy, I accept that my fate is to feel things. And that... has to be ok. I will change the world, small bites, then big bites, internally and externally...And for all of those who scoff at my audacity to want to do so, I say this...

I will.

Check my mirror.

Chapter 6

What's in your pockets, brother?

Lint, a small pocket knife, two quarters, three pennies, a lighter and an almost worn down lip balm. When I worked at my corporate job, that was common. Then, a few years after that, I went out on my own and started my own business. I was in sales for the most part. We all are. Every day. I carried with me five paperclips in my left pocket. Every sale I went on, every person I talked to that day about my business was represented by one paperclip moved to my right pocket. I would not finish my day until they all jumped from my left pocket to my right.

From March until May, on most days it was practice plans or lineup cards that found a home in my pockets. And a pen to make changes. Always a pen. Then there was teaching. My keys to my office and my phone were kept in my front right pocket until class was over. I didn't like them to fall out or take up space, although when I sat, if they dug in, I would place them on the desk in my classroom. Then there is nothing, just a place for my hand when it gets tired of hanging there. As of this last weekend, I added something to my pocket. I am carrying around my FTRN creed that I wrote out and carry with me. Just reaching in and touching it, no matter what I am doing, gives to me a serene calm that washes over me, one fiber of my being at a time. I feel like I am home.

The Great Depression was a time and place I have only read about in an eighth grade history class and maybe heard a few stories about once or twice from my grandmother harping on how bad things were when she and my grandfather were younger. There seemed always to be something to harp on…how they stood in line for bread or how when times were really rough, they put cardboard box tops in their shoes to make them last longer when they would wear out. I think I have heard my mother tell that same story. Or how I was out late the night before and made sure my mom knew what time I came in, or the fact that my elbows were on the table at some point last week. Oh, Nana, God bless you…may you rest in peace.

Bing Crosby sang a song written in 1931 during the depression. You may have heard of it… "Brother, can you spare a dime?" It goes like this:

"They used to tell me I was building a dream, and so I followed the mob. When there was earth to plow, or guns to bear, I was always there right on the job. They used to tell me I was building a dream, with peace and glory ahead, Why should I be standing in line, just waiting for bread? Once I built a railroad, I made it run, made it race against time. Once I built a railroad; now it's done. Brother, can you spare a dime?"

This seems relatable in these times. Things are hard for some people. Money is hard to come by. Jobs are few. Extra is not normal. I think, though, it is so much more about what we choose to do with the money we have. What we choose to spend our dimes on. What we choose to spend our time on. It's all a choice. Obviously, when you have it to make choices about. We also choose what we can spare, what we feel we can give out into the universe on any given day. The "dime" doesn't have to be money. It can be your heart … your words of inspiration, your gift of love to someone who needs it today. So I am wondering…

What's in your pockets? And can you spare any of it? Is it holding you down? Is it what you need to survive tomorrow? Can you give it away? Or is it even what you WANT? OR... are your pockets empty?

Maybe tomorrow, you will try replacing the emptiness of your pockets with a picture of your baby while you are at work to remind you of your WHY. Maybe you will make a "to do" list and carry it around with you so you can make sure you get to everything you need to do.

Maybe you can find a way to make a healthy grocery list instead of just walking in and buying whatever jumps off the shelf at you when you are hungry. OR, perhaps you will write down the FTRN creed and carry that with you, too. So you can find new inspirations during the day to be audacious, to see yourself and others... to be a nexus, to follow the Kaizen path - to change the world, one piece of lint, one paperclip, one penny, one moment at a time. It's all we have. It's our choice. What you put in your pockets is what you carry with you every day. YOU get to choose that.

Choose wisely.

So I will ask you again... what's in YOUR pockets, Brother?

And can you spare a dime?

Chapter 7

Don't expect, but be ready.

I had someone ask me the other day how I know what to write about… how my blogs come to be. I thought about that and answered with one word: Awareness. I think maybe I travel through life with my eyes wide open. I allow the things I see and hear around me connect to my mind and my heart. I challenge how they relate to life, the little things especially. They are my favorite moments. You can learn a lot about life by watching a small child in a grocery store

I was standing near the blueberries, when a little girl, maybe five or six, was standing tall in her pretty red dress and black patent leather shoes. Daddy was starting to walk toward the checkout lanes but noticed she wasn't following him. She was standing there staring at the caramel apple kit and pleading, "Daddy, Daddy… I want this, I want it." "Let's go, Maddy. We need to get home, we are already late," he replied in a hurry.

She wasn't budging. I put some berries in my cart and started to turn around when her shrill demands got louder. "DADDY, What is this? Is it the same thing?? I WANT SOME!" Daddy stopped the cart about 10 feet away, turned around and walked over to her as she was getting louder and louder shouting "Daddy" about five times a second. He smiled as he passed me and said… "I should have been ready for that. She LOVES caramel apples. We used to make them at Grandma's house when she was still alive."

I smiled and I think I let out an "Awwww" as he passed me. He knelt down to Maddy's level and told her they were going to be late and that they already had something to make special apples at home. She smiled at him with a huge, tearful smile and put her arms up to him to be picked up. He was gracious, kind and loving as he lifted her into the cart. Off they went, late for wherever they were supposed to be.

I smiled quietly and walked toward the registers myself.

Expectations can be tricky. As an athlete, they can be damaging to your confidence levels during play. The issue is that when we expect something to happen and it doesn't, we are disappointed, or we see ourselves as a failure. Expectations set us up to fail. One of the factors that help us build confidence is preparation…being ready.

I talk to athletes all the time about this. And I realized in the Giant the other day that Maddy's dad understood the concept, too. I noticed he didn't say anything about expecting little Maddy to throw a fit because she wanted the caramel apple kit. He said… "I should have been ready for it."

We never know how those we love will react to news we tell them, good or bad, or when we do something they may or may not agree with. If we expect something and we get the opposite, we are often disappointed. When we are just there, accepting of whatever the response is… ready to hear it, regardless of what it is… we will never be disappointed.

I have learned to really make that a way of life. No expectations.

But I am ready.

As is Maddy, to make those special apples.

Chapter 8

Who's in your front row?

Timing is everything. Change is good. I am doing a front row check.

I was driving home tonight from South Jersey after visiting a client. It was almost 10 o'clock. I was on the phone; then I took a minute to randomly check what song was on my iPod. I turned up the volume. Right then, the very haunting first track on one of the Shinedown albums came on. The song is actually a poem written by one of the band members and recited by his daughter. It's called "The Dream."

I sat and took it in. I got a chill up my spine. I LOVE when I have moments connect like that. There is so much you can take from those lines… And as an English major in college, my Senior Seminar was an advanced poetry class that you had to apply to and be accepted into. MOST times I get poetry, and other times I don't. And either way, like all art forms, it is allowed to be interpreted. People are allowed to have viewpoints. They are also allowed to be wrong.

Sometimes, we do not even realize who we are surrounding ourselves with until we stop to realize that these are not the same people we had set out to find. The start that has no end, choosing the right people to be your friends, … it's all more and more clear for me…why I was reminded of these two things today.

We show up, we watch, we listen, we give our input, and we go home. We buy the front row seat to someone else's show. And we GIVE AWAY the tickets to our own.

Sometimes, just maybe, we should raise our own price. We should build a velvet rope around our stand-by line. We should create a VIP list. We should say NO, I'm sorry, but those seats are reserved. The only option is the balcony. We should arrange them the way WE want them; after all, it's our theater.

It's our show.

It's our life.

The ones who sit the closest get to see your imperfections, get spit on by accident, but sometimes get to hear you the clearest. They are the only ones who can touch you that easily.

Tell me, are the people who are the closest to you the right ones?

Did they earn that right? Did they pay the price?

Or did you give it away for free?

Pay attention. Choose wisely.

Give and take. Evenly.

Be front-row worthy.

And keep searching for the right people to keep close.

Keep searching for the start that has no end.

And then tell me… when you are brave and ready.

Who's in YOUR front row?

Part Two.

Love.

"I have known love because I live it. I have felt love because I give it. I can receive love because it's the only thing that breathes life into my soul. I love. I am love."
—jlc

She unfurled her brow for a minute to ask him yet again...
"Why can't love just be enough to mend broken things?"
Silence.
She looked back to see if he was listening to her. Or really, to see if he was even there to hear her question.
His head was cocked to the side, his eyes squinted in deep thought. After three minutes and 47 seconds, his voice softer than she had ever heard it... answered slowly.
"How broken are the things?"
She was taken aback by the response.
"Huh?" was all she could muster out... "How broken are what things?"
She had no idea what he was getting at...
After all it was a few minutes after she muttered what her

heart was feeling, perhaps not really processing it with her
head enough to know what she even said in the first place.
Rambling thoughts...
She looked at him again.
He was now sitting... pondering the magnitude of the
question she didn't even know she asked.
"You asked why love can't be enough to mend broken things...
I wanted to know how broken they are in the first place."
She nodded... "Oh yeah..." slowly remembering why she asked.
Her body was aching that day. The cold was setting in and
making her muscles remind her that they existed.
Her head was still pounding.
Her parents were not well. Her idea of where she would be at
the age of 39 was not at all where she was.
Broken in some places... days of feeling broken in all of them.
She just wanted to know.
Isn't love the answer...?
"I don't know how broken, I mean..."
He scoffed back all of a sudden in a deeper, louder voice.
"NO... that wasn't a real question. I wasn't asking you
to really tell me the degree of brokenness you feel. I was
asking you to understand that anything that feels broken
is perspective. You are choosing to see that part of it. Stop
feeling sorry for yourself, dammit."
Stop...
A slow rolling tear appeared off the corner of her left eye,
quickly smeared by the light blue sleeve of her hooded jacket.
She wanted no parts of him seeing that.
After all, she had some feelings that he was right.
"Just stop." She whispered to herself in a deep moan, like she
wanted to get it out, but it got trapped in her right lung as the
air grew heavier again.
He didn't say another word.
She got it.
Love was her only focus. Today, tomorrow... she would find
all the ways love existed. And she would tell him all about it.
...as soon as she fixed her broken keyboard.

Chapter 9

I now know love's beauty...

Not a time I would choose. Or ever yearn for. Not the loss or the emptiness that comes with it would I ask for. But my heart finds its way through the endless aches and pains because the beauty of simple love, of what love truly represents and stands for was shown to me at 12:34 last Saturday afternoon. My sweet baby girl Macy took her last three breaths. Audible for me to hear, yet gentle enough for me to feel calmed by.

She was one of my three dogs. One of the two I rescued to a better life. The one who made me laugh with her laid back, eyes half closed demeanor. The dog who could lay her head all the way back behind her, who would always keep a paw on you to remind you she was there. The dog who stole my heart...and I didn't even know it.

She was my lesson in patience, in sweetness, in unconditional love. I would yell at her, she would wag her tail faster. I would come home from a miserable day and she would be literally bent in half, wagging her tail so hard, I think it actually, at times, wagged her. We called her "wiggles" because of her ability to be so excited, her body would curl, and her tail would smack herself in the face. She was always squinting because of it.

She started to get sick in May... I noticed she wasn't eating as much and was losing weight. But the truth is, if I didn't notice that stuff, I wouldn't have known anything. She still was excited to see me when I walked in, wiggling and carrying on as usual. The first few steps out the door on a walk were my favorite. She couldn't walk in a straight line, she was so excited... She snorted like a little pig, the tail going in sporadic circles we called "helicopter tail" and her prance became quick and bouncy.

In every moment, even to the last three breathes, my sweet baby girl loved life. And she taught me a lot about it...

Macy was going to be put down back in 2003 when I adopted her. She was left on the side of the road with her sister and both were saved from a high-kill shelter in North Carolina and brought to a rescue in PA. I saw her online and immediately knew I needed to meet this sweet face. I attended a meet and greet on a Sunday in the summer of 2003 in the park with dogs from all different shelters and organizations. I saw her sitting under a tent, eyes barely open because the sun was so bright. After a few minutes talking with the ladies there, I picked her up. She laid peacefully in my arms and squinted up at me. She licked me... one of Macy's traits... that long tongue that always snipered guests in my house. I knew I had to have her.

The next day the ladies from the animal placement agency called me and told me they would like to have me bring my beagle for a visit to see how they get along. I did. And they did. Macy came home with me a few days later.

That first night, Zoe and Macy fell asleep together on the couch. I knew she fit right in. It was easy. She was love... pure and simple. Love in every turn. And the feeling was mutual.

I could go on and on about the stories that made us laugh and cry... the ways she lit up the room and the ways she made me love her... But the one truth remains... her love was simple and it was pure.

On Saturday, as I sit in the room waiting for the doctor to come and administer the injection, I held Macy in my arms. Just like the first day I fell in love with her. The last day, I held her and fell in love with her all over again. She nestled herself against me, so gentle and sweet. I thought, "how perfect. She came into my life in my arms… she gets to leave the same way." The tears flowed. As the injection started, she rested her head in the crook of my arm, so warm and gentle. I kissed her head and told her I loved her… that she was the best girl in the world. I told her it was ok to go. With three audible breaths, she went peacefully.

If it's possible that death can be beautiful, I felt it on Saturday at 12:34pm. Her grace and peace hugged me as she left her physical body. I felt a strange peacefulness through my tears. That day I was flooded with well wishes and emails from friends and family. I appreciated every single one. But one stood out to me… It was the Rainbow Bridge poem that owners of pets often get when they go through loss. It didn't stand out because I had never seen it before… I had. But that evening, when I was leaving dinner with a friend, on my way to speak at a field hockey camp… I walked out of the restaurant and looked up. After a quick five-minute rainstorm, there appeared the most beautiful rainbow I have seen in a long while. I knew she had sent that to me to let me know she was there, waiting.

Macy taught me a lot about love, and about life… about peace and calm, about gentleness and about the pure beauty of letting go. I will remember her eyes, the love that she spoke through them, the heartbeat I felt when I held her close in those last minutes. Love is beautiful.

She showed me in ways I would have never known.

Chapter 10

It's the process, not outcome...

Begin with the end in mind. Know where you want to go.

What is your personal journey? What path are you walking down? Is it the path less traveled, or is it a well-worn street? Where are you on your journey?

So often, we worry about our plans for tomorrow... or we waste so much time planning for our future. Am I about to tell you not to? NO. I'm a planner, a dreamer, a wisher. I always like to set goals and strive to achieve each and every one of them. So, no ... I am not telling you to stop all of that. That would be crazy...

Or would it?

I often think about this and have internal fights with myself. I have asked these same questions of my athletes who sit in the chairs in my office, I have asked coaches and players, parents and kids... I have asked myself. I have looked in the mirror and asked.

I have gotten every answer I could find. So what? ... What is it about goal setting and planning for the future that hangs us all up? What is it that freezes us sometimes to take action?

I have started to get really good at living in the moment. I learned it the hard way. I have lost a lot in my life, and I know I will continue to do so as I get older. I have learned how to let go of the tangible. I have spent hours in Barnes and Noble reading, soul searching, finding ME. In many of those moments, I never even knew I was lost. Why do we have such a hard time just letting go and letting things happen in our lives? Why do we suffer from the need to control the outcome?

I see it in the athletes I serve. Many of them are so worried about stats and wins/losses, and what the end result will be that they forget to play the game. And as a result, they play poorly. So instead, we work on playing in the moment. We talk about three of my mantra words: Be. Here. Now.

Have you ever been truly present? Really? Have you ever really been in the moment, with no worries about the past or future? You were there... every thought and action devoted to 3:52 on a Tuesday afternoon in October of 2011. And then when 3:52 was over, you gave everything you could to 3:53... knowing that you will never live it again. What I have found is that we never get these moments back... and when we lose people in our lives, it's another minute closer to the reality that we will all die someday. I'm sorry if that seemed like a slap in the face, but it's real and honest. We are so afraid to talk about death because we have a hard time accepting it. But as soon as we learn to let go of outcome and focus solely on our present moment, the fear is gone. We aren't afraid of what we don't know because we aren't focused there. We give everything we have to everything we do. And it becomes good enough.

So we push on... and even if 3:54 isn't a good minute, or even a productive one, we trade it for another one, and so on.

This is the process of truly living. This is what we forget how to do so often...

We worry so much about the end result – the outcome - that we forget to live... WHY?

It's like all the people I know who wish away five days of the week just to have two on the weekend. Why do we do that? I can't say that I do that myself, however, because all seven days of the week are the same to me. I do what I love with people I enjoy to be around... so I never wish any of my days away. Is it time to question that habit? Perhaps I am just being real today. And if this is hard to read, if you find you are adjusting yourself to find a comfortable spot in your seat, then good. I got the response I was looking for - because in reality, these moments that you don't get back, they are all that you have. Don't waste them or wish them away. Trade them for something worthwhile.

After all is said and done, it's the process not the outcome that matters.

Now you know...

Is it time for a mirror test? Take a moment to look at yourself in the mirror.

Make sure you are happy with what you see when you look into your own eyes.

How are you living your time?

You have this minute right now to use how you wish. Don't waste it.

It's 4:01p.m., Tuesday, October 26, 2011. This is the only one we get.

Trade it wisely. Then let it go.

It's now 4:02.

Chapter 11

And above all else... Love

It's a simple thought really, one that I could end on before I started writing. But so many times recently, I got myself thinking about what Love really is. Why there is so much to say about it. And why we often fear it, and accuse it of being too "soft" most of the time.

I opened up a folding chair and put it next to Helen as her daughter Carolyn was feeding her lunch. The Tuesday routine is simple. The sectioned plate full of pureed chicken or turkey or whatever it is that day. Mashed potatoes or mac and cheese. Also pureed. And veggies, of course. Like baby food. We have to read the slip attached to the tray to know what they are because it is sometimes difficult to tell just by looking at the plate. And then there's dessert. Always dessert. No resident skips that part. Like the child inside who couldn't wait for the end of the meal, the dessert is the best part. Helen looked bright-eyed and awake last Tuesday. She made a satisfactory noise at every spoonful of Jello she swallowed. It was easily the highlight of her day.

I just sat and smiled as both she and my mom ate their red Jello. When Carolyn came back from throwing something away, Helen was still eating. She smiled with red teeth and lips and reached out to grab my arm. As she did, she looked at Carolyn and said, "this is my friend, and I love her."

For some reason, a rush of emotion came over me, and I had to choke back the tears.

So simple. So sweet and real. Helen knows nothing about me. She doesn't even really know who I am there visiting or who I am. She just knows that I am her friend. She recognizes me as someone who smiles and laughs with her. And that seems to be enough.

Love. That honest and true feeling of connection. A self-giving emotion that creates more of it as it moves through itself. Love creates more love. I don't know what my first memory of it is or how it came to be a very real part of my existence, but I know of it well.

Growing up as a preacher's kid, I equated a lot of what I learned about love to church services and family. I remember when I was in middle school, one of my favorite church services was Maundy (Holy) Thursday. It was the night before Good Friday during Easter weekend. The service started rather normally, but ended in a way that has always intrigued me. In the middle of the service, my dad would always get on his knees with a bowl of water and invite anyone who wanted to, to come up and sit in the chair and get their "feet washed." It was a very symbolic way of cleansing, stripping away all of the impurities, getting ready for Good Friday. It was also a way for others to come and take my dad's place in a servant role, kneeling in front of those who wanted to be cleansed. I always wanted to go up front and participate. It seemed so simple, so loving, such a symbolic way of serving others and allowing them to serve in my healing.

I always regretted not doing it. I wasn't sure I was worthy. I think back now and it almost seems silly to think I wasn't old enough. I knew love. That is all that mattered really. I guess I didn't realize then how much I really understood it.

After that part of the service, slowly and quietly, the altar would be stripped by the older women in the church who would take away the flowers and the candles and the silver. They removed the draped cloths and decorative pieces one by one. The church would get darker throughout and it would become perfectly quiet and still. In the darkness, you could make out a barren altar where there once was life. The cross was even covered with black mesh draping. Death was moving in as Good Friday was upon us. This was a very moving service, and I would always see tears in my mom's eyes as we slipped out quietly to make our way to the back room where we would soon greet everyone after the service.

This would be what we called "Agape"… our representation of the last supper. The table would be lined with cups of red wine in the shape of a fish, the tail lined with grape juice for those of us who weren't old enough to partake in the wine. In the middle of the fish was a long, braided piece of bread. As people came into the room, we would break bread with them as a sign of love, or agape. We shared bread with each other, also sharing a love that seemed so simple. The funny thing is that I never really knew what "agape" meant until one night, on our walk down the hill to our house from the church, I asked my dad. We were carrying the leftover bread and bottles of grape juice and wine. The darkness surrounded me with emotion again that night. And he told me that "agape" meant love, a selfless kind of love that is shown when we give of ourselves, when we serve others without thinking of what we may get back. It meant loving all of humanity, regardless of their place in our lives or their status in society.

That simple definition sparked a conversation as we walked in the door and put down the bags. We stood in the kitchen talking about how deep that love could go. We talked about what it meant to love unselfishly, unconditionally. I told him I knew. He and my mom gave that kind of love to me every day. I was 13 and felt like I understood. Easily and simply, love just was. There was never a question.

I feel the simple love of a woman who doesn't really know her own name, as she touched my arm last Tuesday and called me her friend. And the deep love of my parents who taught me the simple act of Agape. And the love that stretches in between from those I don't know and smile at as I pass, to the homeless man I gave $20 to so he could have a roof over his head for a night. And the love I feel when I look at the cherry blossom tree in my front yard today to the love I see in my dogs eyes as he falls asleep on the couch next to me as I write this.

Love is simple and deep. It is strong and true. It is scary and soft and difficult to understand all in the same breath.

It is all I know. It is all I am and all I ever want to be.
Unselfish and strong.
Simple and true.

Chapter 12

Take it Slow... No Regrets.

A couple weeks ago, Monday started out with a feeling of fear. I am often shaken when I see a car accident... or at least the remnants of one. I was stopping by the Dunkin Donuts in town to get my decaf coffee, my morning ritual. I turned into the parking lot and actually saw what was causing the traffic...a minivan, ripped apart, pieces of what was once the inside strewn about the road. I knew the driver wasn't ok after seeing the state of the vehicle. I remember back to when I was 16, the car accident that has left me with a chronic pain condition all these years later. One split second can change your life. My parents' biggest nightmare... the phone call at 11:30 pm telling them that their daughter is in the hospital. The frantic rush to get in their car and get there. I know it all too well. That Monday a couple weeks ago came with one of those phone calls to the family of that minivan driver. It also came with a phone call to me.

My mom has been battling a very progressive neurological disorder called Cortico Basal Degeneration for the better part of eight years now, and she has been declining quite steadily lately. She can't communicate very well, she can't bathe herself, she can't get to the bathroom alone or even walk. She needs someone to feed her, to move her, to pretty much do everything for her now. It has been a long and very emotional road for our family. Monday turned out to be another bump in that road and a reminder of what it is to love unconditionally, and more importantly… to love simply.

I received a call that mom was taken to the hospital. Pneumonia had set it. I rushed out of my office to get there to be with my family. It was raining. And as my feet hit the embankment that led to the parking lot, they gave out. I slid down the hill in the mud.

I didn't have time to even wipe myself off.

Without hesitation, I got up and with a tear fighting my cheek, I climbed into my truck. We were all thinking the worst.

She got through that with a few days in the hospital. The doctors said that despite her brain fighting her, her heart was strong.

I sat one afternoon in the hospital, reading to her. I sent my Dad home for a nap and my sisters had to go pick up the kids from school. I took a walk downstairs to the gift shop to find a book to read. I came across some kind of inspirational book with short stories. I bought it and went back upstairs. When I went in, mom was in and out of sleep, dozing on and off. When she opened her eyes and looked at me, I asked her if she wanted me to read to her. She got excited and said yes. I pulled a chair up next to the bed and started to read, resting one hand on her hand and using the other to turn the pages of the book in my lap. I read to her for the better part of an hour. We laughed at some of the names in the book as well as at each other. Just to laugh.

It was a wonderful time that I won't soon forget. It was simple. It was pure. I was lost for an hour just BEING. I hadn't done that in a long time, and it felt great.

We sat in silence for some of the time, too, as if we just wanted to sit together. I loved every second of it regardless of why we were there.

The simple joy of unspoken love was enough.

Chapter 13

Tell her I said hi…

I was leaving the event, tired and not looking forward to the long drive home. I wasn't sure what to say anyway. Maybe I will just walk by and pretend I didn't see her. No luck. I feel her tug my left jacket sleeve twice. "Hi, Jen."

"Hi… How are you doing?" I asked hesitantly.

"Ok, I guess. Or as good as could be expected."

"I'm very sorry to hear about your mom." I choked back a tear that seemed to travel to my throat instead of finding its way out of my right eye. Thankfully, she wouldn't see it there. God knows I wasn't really opening my mouth very much.

I hate talking about death. I hate losing people. I guess I don't fear it; I just am tired of talking about it.

I guess…

Fear is a funny word. I think I just let it become more of a nuisance than anything. And I change the subject. A lot. I thought about the last time I saw her mom. She looked frail and thin. She was so pretty.

I looked down at my phone and told her I had to run... I was going to be late. For what, I don't know... but I knew it would allow me to leave without feeling rude.

If I was rude, I didn't notice. And I hoped she didn't either.

Time is always the best excuse. Another tear got trapped in my throat... waiting to see if it was free to flow out. "NO." I made sure it heard me. The picture of my mom on my phone came up when I checked the time. Her beautiful smile. Her gorgeous eyes. I turned to leave. Tear in the throat number three...

Again, that tug. This time my right sleeve.

"How's your mom, Jen?" "Tell her I said Hi..." There it was. The dreaded request.

"I will. Thanks."

Off I hurried... to nowhere in particular.

I went out to my car and sat there. Wondering where I was going to go, I looked at my phone again. Her eyes told me a story.

This time, the tear found the corner of my eye. I kept fighting.

After 18 minutes, I started driving.

To nowhere in particular, I was doing 68 in a 55. I was on a mission. To nowhere. Maybe it was me being lost. Maybe I just wanted everything to go back to "normal"...

Maybe I had a need to see or hear or touch her.

Maybe, it was just that I wasn't sure where I was going and felt like I would figure it out if I drove faster...

Maybe I was just in denial.

Life continued to whiz by me, tractor-trailers and buses in the right lane beside me. I felt like I was standing still.

Tell her I said hi…

Part of me wanted to say, no… YOU tell her. But instead, I just hurried off so as not to be late.

For something. Nothing. Anything.

I just wanted to get out of the grasp of the tug.

So much of the beginning stages of my understanding my mom's disease was denial. It was the realization that at the age of 29, I was told my mom was going to die a slow death in front of my eyes and I couldn't do anything but watch it happen. I just wanted to get away from it all. I ran, I drove, I kept my mouth closed for a couple years. I cried choked up tears and silent sobs. I wanted to make it all go away.

I wanted to hurry up and be ok with the process.

I barely went to visit. I was scared of what it would look like.

I didn't want to be the one to tell her anyone said hi, let alone me.

Then it hit me…

I can't control the outcome… but what I can control is my process through it.

I can control how I react to it and what I do to make it easier. Driving home that night, I took a detour.

I drove straight to my parents instead. I wanted to see her. I wanted to be there. I wanted her to know I didn't really run away. I just was "Busy." And when I had enough, I would leave because I was busy. I have kept busy. I have hurried along from place to place. But one thing that has changed in my process of growing through all of it is my ability to just be there, to just be present.

I am busier than ever and I have seen my mom more lately than I have since she's been sick.

I am comfortable where I am with the process.

And I tell her hi... every time I see her.
Usually at least 18 times.

Perhaps we see things that aren't really there.
She thought this to be true but wasn't really sure of anything anymore.
"Do you ever get tired of feeling so much?"
She asked aimlessly, not thinking there would really be a response.
After all, there usually isn't when she needs one and always is when she doesn't really want to know the truth.
Maybe this was a little of both.
She closed her eyes and started to wonder if there was something better.
Something more.
Something that would tug on her soul and burn that fire in her gut again.
She felt it once on an idle Tuesday at 4:13 in the afternoon when she was supposed to be doing something else.
Perhaps she felt this burning because she wanted to, not because it really existed.
But then again, this was more of her not wanting to be right.
What if she was so much more...?
"I don't know what you mean." His voice boomed over the slight wind that was blowing north to southeast across the tall grass, making it shake like her foot when she is lost in thought.
How is anything considered "too much?"
Who decides these things?
She closed her eyes and allowed the wind to take her breath away.

Chapter 14

Mommy, why are you crying?

My big blue eight-year-old eyes looked up at mom in the candlelight. The sounds of instruments and choir voices filled the walls from the front to the back of the church. Well, I assumed it did. I didn't know anything about the back of the church. I actually knew nothing other than the front pew, first seat. It would be mine for at least 11 years.

I watched as a tear flowed down her cheek. And then another. "Mommy, why are you crying?" I whispered quietly, just loud enough for her to hear me, but not too loud to interrupt the flute six feet away. Her light blue eyes reached down to me, held me for a moment and then answered. "Because the music is so beautiful," she whispered back with a gentleness that made me feel in that moment that I may cry too. The music. The voice of the soloist was piercing. It was mom's favorite Christmas song. And to this day when I hear it, I can't often hold back the tears.

Mom always made sure she was in that front pew by 9:30 every Christmas Eve so she wouldn't miss the music. I didn't understand what was so special about it. I mean, it was only instruments and people singing, often in other languages. I couldn't really understand what they were saying, which made it harder for me to connect. But I sat there, quietly, listening, watching as Mom would cry every year. I would reach out and hold her hand, thinking that at least I could console her somehow. When I was eight, tears meant sadness. I needed to just hold her hand.

Mom and I had a ritual. When it came time for the sermon, I would lean over onto her left arm and she would run her fingernails over my arms to tickle them while we listened to dad talk. It wasn't odd for me to listen to Dad talk, and often I wasn't sure at eight years old really what he was talking about, so I just enjoyed the time Mom would spend rubbing my arms. Dad's words were often as powerful as the music and the voices. When I would see a tear on Mom's cheek, I knew it must have been a good one... whatever he was talking about. I would reach out and hold her hand. She would squeeze it back.

The second part of our ritual was after the sermon and the prayers and before communion. It was the Lord's Prayer. That was our time. When I was really young and learning how to read, I would kneel in front of her and she would run my finger over the words in the prayer book so I could follow along. Some days, my finger would almost burn from all the words we rubbed it across because we would do all the prayers that way. Other days, it was just the Lord's Prayer. After a while when I was older, she would reach out and hold my hand instead. For years, we held hands during the Lord's Prayer. Even after I turned 30. No matter where I was in relation to her in the pew, or even in the pew behind her... she would turn and look for me and reach out her hand. That was our time. The connection I had with Mom during the Lord's Prayer is something that to this day I acknowledge. Tonight, I held my own hand. And just like after every time, we would squeeze each other's hand and whisper "I love you" at the end. I hope somehow it was enough, and maybe tonight she heard me. There has never been a time after saying the Lord's Prayer that I don't whisper to my mom.

I drove to Reading tonight to sit in the back pew and listen to Dad. I went early to make sure I was there for the music. I sat at the end of the pew. First seat. As the procession started to the classic first song on Christmas Eve - O Come all Ye Faithful -I stood and sang in the pew alone. As the cross and the choir passed, Dad would bring up the rear. As he got to where I was sitting, he reached out his hand to squeeze mine on his way by. I squeezed back. A tear flowed down my cheek as I whispered, "I love you."

I sat and listened to the music. I felt all of it. I listened to Dad's sermon. The tears flowed. No arm rubs or hand squeezes. No pew so packed with family that we had to spill into the two behind us. No laughing so hard that the floor would shake. A totally different experience as life changes year by year. A quiet solitude that brought introspection and a deep love for all that I miss.

As I drove home, I listened to Christmas music. I looked at all the Christmas lights I passed and the beautiful luminaries that some streets had lit. And then, when I was five miles away, it came on the radio. That song. Mom's favorite Christmas song. One of my favorite renditions, of course. Josh Groban was singing O, Holy Night. I sang with him. And through the tears, I could see mom's eyes looking back at me. And for a moment, I felt peace. Because the music is so beautiful.

I get it now. "I love you Mom."

Merry Christmas.

Chapter 15

When your cup is full...

When I heard his voice at the other end say hello, I smiled. My heart sped up. I felt so happy to reconnect. "Maurice?" I said, hoping it was really him. "Yes... who is this?" he responded hesitantly. "Maurice, it's Jen. Jen Croneberger." I could hear a second of silence, then a sound of joy/emotion/pure love come through the phone. "JEN, Oh my goodness. Is it really you? I can't believe it's you."

I couldn't stop smiling the entire 14-minute conversation on my ride home from West Chester this afternoon. I found him. My long lost friend for whom I had not been able to locate a phone number for over a year and a half. Our connection was so strong and pure that we talked as if we had just talked yesterday.

Maurice is like family to me. He and his wife lost their daughter to a stray bullet aimed for someone else seven years ago. I sat in the Wilmington courtroom every day during the murder trial as the court saw an innocent family lose an innocent daughter, the mother of two innocent young boys. Maurice and Narda would now have to raise them. They lived in a tough neighborhood, struggling to get by. Life had not been easy for them; they lived paycheck to paycheck for most of their existence.

Maurice was battling health issues and couldn't work much. They did without what a lot of people would think are non-negotiables. There wasn't a time during these past 12 years that I doubted Maurice's faith. Our conversations were often about how good God is. Never doubting, never questioning. With very little of what most people would see as necessities for a good life, Maurice and Narda's cup was, is and always will be full. They don't want for much.

In all the years I have known Maurice, I have to say that he is probably the most positive, full of hope and faith human being that I have known. The only thing he always talked about was being able to one day buy his family a house.

It was maybe a minute into our conversation today when he told me he was calling all the numbers he had for me but couldn't find me. He could not wait to share the news. He and Narda had finally bought that house he had been talking about forever just this past year. They moved into a nicer, safer neighborhood for the boys, and he told me, as always, how blessed he is and how good God is.

I couldn't stop smiling. He told me he wanted me there for the housewarming party but couldn't find me. He told me I would be so proud of them. I smiled from ear to ear. I WAS proud. Maurice and Narda are like family to me. The one dream they have had for 30 years has come true. I couldn't help but cry as I sat at the red light at Bondsville Road by the Turkey Hill. I am so happy for them. We promised I would come see the new house over Christmas, and I could see how big the boys are getting. I miss them too. He told me that they still play the game I got them for Christmas a few years ago. But now, it's different. Now, they can sit together around a table and eat dinner and play games as a family. They never had a dining room table that they could sit around before. He made sure he mentioned that to me. That is what he is most thankful for. A table where he and his family would be able to sit around all at once – together.

I hung up, remembering my love for this man and his family. Feeling it stronger than ever. Knowing how much he contributes to the world by just being him.

Then I started to think about what it says in the Tao. "When your cup is full, stop pouring."

We so often want more than we currently have. We make lists of all the things we don't have that we feel we need in order to live the life we want. We buy more clothes than we can wear at any given time. We fill our closets until they are spitting things out. We have an excess of… stuff. We buy bigger houses and fancier cars, and we think it means something. We want more. Always searching for more. Thinking these things will fulfill us.

But do they? Does another pair of shoes make us feel better about ourselves? When we think about it, we can wear only one pair at a time. The others just sit there. And of course, there are those who have none. We keep pouring. And our cup overflows. We waste. We mop it up. And we pour some more.

Maybe we should just stop. All of us. I am just as guilty as anyone. I have overstuffed closets, more books than I could ever take time to read again, when really, what I want my cup to be full of is the feeling I had during those 14 minutes on the phone today. Of a faith and a love so strong that it lasted all day. Of a reminder that life really is good, regardless of the things we go through. That love is enough. We don't need much more.

And what a more perfect day than today, December 1st, to spend some time with this on our hearts?. Today is World Aids day. A day when we remember those who have gone before us, those who suffer silently and not so silently with this fateful disease that we still battle on this earth.

Today also happens to be "Pay it Forward Day" in the social networking world. Today, we take a moment to maybe think about those around us in ways we have maybe neglected. We give back by giving forward. We do something random for a stranger, even a smile that maybe brightens their day. We give. Whatever it is. Today also begins seven days of the "Love is Louder" project, a project that reminds us that love is louder than any negative anyone could say or do to bring us down. We rally together for these next seven days to remember those who maybe feel like they don't fit in, or who are bullied, made fun of or made to feel small. We give. Whatever it is. December 1st is a great day to begin a new journey then, it seems. To give back, to say thank you, to stand up for those who are scared or silent, to stand by those who are affected by AIDS or HIV, to hold the door for someone, to pay it forward. To stop pouring in our own cups that are overflowing, and turn and fill someone else's. What a great day to be on this earth.

My cup is very full. I am ready to share. Are you?

Yes, sir, my brother Maurice. God is good.

Thank you for reminding me

Chapter 16

Heart of all things... LOVE.

I am sure there isn't a person out there who doesn't remember what they were doing at 8:46 a.m. on September 11, 2001. That day changed us all. And every year at this time, I can recall how it felt on that gorgeous September morning. These beautiful days, blue skies, crisp mornings... All remind me of driving up to Princeton, New Jersey, early that Tuesday to babysit my 18-month-old nephew, Palmer.

I was helping my sister and her husband that summer a few days a week so they didn't have to do the daycare thing yet. I got there around 8:20 that morning, in time to say goodbye to my brother-in-law and ready to do breakfast with Palmer. I was planning to spend the day with him outside, going for a walk, and playing with his favorite soccer ball. It was a day just like any other day. I talked to my sister on the phone for a few minutes as she was telling me how she would decide that daycare was the only option. She was upset and felt badly that they didn't have a way to keep him at home. She knew I had to get back to my business in Delaware, and they needed to make the tough decision. That phone call could have saved her life.

See, what I have not told you is that my sister Rebecca is an attorney for the Port of Authority of New York and New Jersey. Her office was on the 61st floor of the World Trade Center... Tower number 1. And yes, she was there that day... sitting at her desk when the first plane hit just above her. It shook the building so hard, her door slammed shut and she had to find her way out. Without hesitation, she made her way to the stairs and began her journey down, passing firefighters and police on their way up who knew that they might never make the trek back down. She made her way out of the building and to my brother's apartment about a mile away. Through the streets she ran, covered in ash. At the same time, we sat dialing and redialing over and over, just to hear her voice. Three long hours had passed before we knew she was alive.

That day, for all involved, was a labor of love. It was a day that we tested the strength of our ability to reach out and understand, to find new ways to appreciate each other. To love, regardless of the barriers we once held onto.

That day changed us all. We became a country of people who loved each other overnight. American flags flew everywhere. People held doors again. We embraced strangers. We smiled more - all through tragedy and loss. 2,993 people lost their lives that day for us to remember to be kind and gentle to each other. And I knew some personally. Yet, regardless of whether or not you were personally affected by loss that day, you were a part of the "kindler, gentler nation" we all witnessed and in which we found solace.

That night, I was given the task of driving to the train station in Princeton to pick up my sister's car she had left there earlier that morning. She was still stuck in the city until they would let people out. As I pulled into the train station parking lot, it occurred to me I wasn't the only one there to pick up a car for someone. I saw tears and fear and so many other emotions I had never seen before. It also occurred to me that some of these cars did not have an owner coming back for them. We were lucky.

On the way home, I stopped at a local sub shop to pick up food. We hadn't really remembered to eat all day. While I was waiting for a large order to feed our family, I sat and watched the day's events unfold on the TV. I was glued to it all day, and sitting in the sub shop with strangers didn't take away the tears. I was mesmerized. I was in shock. I am sure you remember the feeling. And as I sat there, a child, no more than about six or seven years old was running around the shop screaming, playing with his toys. He was loud. VERY loud. And while that would usually grate on me after a short while, I looked at him and smiled. I had no knowledge of what his day was like, and if he had lost anyone that day either. And if he did, did he even know?

And then it hit me… we are so quick to react and to get frustrated with people, and we have no idea what their world is like in that moment.

I am always reminded of the famous quote by the great poet Henry David Thoreau: "Most men lead lives of quiet desperation and go to the grave with the song still in them."

This one day allowed us all to feel the same, and to accept each other for however we chose to be, or not to be.

I want that back. I want to find a better way. I want to not get aggravated at the car driving less than the speed limit in front of me … Maybe there is a reason. I want to not get annoyed at the loud children in the restaurant … Maybe there is a reason. I want to remember that everyone does things differently and it's not always wrong. Because my reminder every year at this time is strong. I want it to be this strong all year. I want us to not have to wait for tragedy to be kind to a stranger… to hold the door … to be more understanding of our shortcomings as human beings.

Because at the heart of all things is love. Always.
How about we find that again?
We are so much stronger that way.

Chapter 17

Never Doubt What is Real...

Growing up, I read a lot. I was also read TO a lot. There were the stories of Uncle Wiggly and Nurse Jane Fuzzy Wuzzy that Mom used to read to me if I was sick or got hurt (which, of course, as an active kid I tended to have my share of injuries), or the Richard Scary books that my brother and I shared and read a lot together. I loved the Hardy Boys and Nancy Drew books. Where the Wild Things Are had a special place in my heart, as did Clifford, The Big Red Dog. But perhaps one of my favorite stories was by Margery Williams... The Velveteen Rabbit.

My dad was an Episcopal Priest (he is now a semi-retired Bishop) and every Sunday found me in the front row on my mom's lap as a small child in church peering up at him as he told stories. At that point, I believed my dad was just a professional storyteller... and in that belief, I definitely wasn't wrong. His sermons were real life stories that related to the message he needed to convey that week. Sometimes they were Charlie Brown and Lucy adventures that made me wonder when Lucy would stop pulling the football out from Charlie Brown's foot as he was about to kick the ball. Other times, he told of angels and sky maidens and hide & seek and Fiddler on the Roof... and of the princess who kissed the frog and turned him into a prince. Yes, Dad, I did listen all those Sundays. And as an adult now, I can finally understand what you were saying all those years ago.

But one story always stood out to me. And every time you used it, I felt deeply what you were saying. Whether I was five or 35, I listened to this story like it was my own.

A young boy was given a stuffed toy rabbit as a Christmas gift, and as it sat in the nursery waiting to be chosen as a playmate, the rabbit wondered what it would take for him to be loved. As he made friends with the other toys in the room, the skin horse explained to him what the goal of all toys is… to be made "real"… and to be loved by a human.

It seemed the rabbit was only worried about the outcome. But the Skin Horse explained to him perhaps in one of the best quotes from the book that "Real isn't how you are made, it's a thing that happens to you."

The rabbit asked the skin horse if it hurts… to which the horse replied, "Yes… sometimes it hurts. But when you are real, you don't mind being hurt."

And that it doesn't happen all at once… It takes time. By the time you are real, you are worn and tattered a bit. But it doesn't matter, because at that point you are really loved. And you can't be ugly… except to people who don't understand.

Doubting what is real is not allowing yourself to open your eyes and your heart to the process. Sometimes we are afraid of what "real" is. Sometimes, we don't really understand why someone else would want to see the "real" in us, both the good and bad, the beautiful and the "ugly"… and usually it's because we don't realize that once we are loved, they see things in us that we may not even know fully exist. They accept us for who we are and even love the worn down parts and the rough patches, droopy ears and sewn-on eyes.

I think it was no coincidence that both of my stuffed animals that I loved the most as a kid have worn out patches and holes. And come to think of it... they are both missing an eye. I think I loved them well.

And I realize now that once that love is there, the doubt disappears.

Never Doubt What Is Real... sometimes you just need to look in the mirror and love who you are anyway. Despite and even through the rough patches.

It's this process of becoming real that I think we all strive for... not so much the outcome.

Droopy ears and all...

Part Three.

Grace

"And there was one last hope to hang onto. The last string that binds my soul to the world. When all else is lost... I find peace in holding on. My peaceful heart knows no other path but grace. I shall travel lightly."
—jlc

She didn't ask for a map. She doesn't even know how to read one. He stuffed it in her face anyway.
"Here... if you want to figure it out, you have to take less turns."
"What is he talking about?" she asked herself for the 17th time.
"Why does everything feel like it's falling apart around me?" she started to mumble out loud.
Her thoughts, obviously starting to wander, and the overwhelming feeling of more than just the map, started to set in. Sinking around her skin like water rushing from a dam... She almost got swept away. Then she remembered it wasn't real.
Back to the map...

"Why are you giving me this? I don't want it." She was getting annoyed. Again.

He barked back... "Because you need it. Don't be stubborn. You will get lost. Take it."

For once, she finally backed down. She knew he was right. She had no idea where the shortcuts were... Or even what the streets looked like or how long they were. No street names, no idea... nothing.

She needed the map.

Maybe she should study it.

Maybe she should accept the fact that she wasn't as smart as he was. That in a race or a competition, he always won. He just knew things.

"You need me..." He said it in almost a quiet, selfless way. A way that caused her to drop all of her walls and defenses.

She accepted this as fact.

And gracefully she reached out to wrap her fingers around the map he was still holding.

She opened it, and as she was about to study it, she saw nothing.

It was blank.

She turned to ask him why he gave her the wrong one...

"You need me" is all she could hear. It echoed for what seemed like hours.

He was gone long before she even opened it...

It was up to her to find her way.

She picked up her colored pencils and began.

Chapter 18

The art of losing gracefully.

Nobody likes to lose. Nobody. It's not fun. It kind of sucks actually. But there are ways to do it that seem to take the sting away a little bit. Even if it's just a little bit. But losing isn't always about the game. Losing is a lot of what happens in life. And losing can be something that is imperative to our long-term well-being. In order to really understand the beauty life gives us, we need to lose.

I watched some of the Women's World Cup games, and I was a fan just like the rest of the country, of our U.S. women's national team. They fought hard. They took a sport in which it is grueling to come back when you are down, and they made it look like something you would see in a movie. They won, they fought hard, and they lost. And in the end, they lost that last game with grace and dignity. They were simply outplayed. There is no shame in that. Sometimes we come up empty. Holding the bag when the bottom falls out. Still, holding the empty bag. They did just that. But they acknowledged the journey. That it was more than the score at the end of the game. They won in intangibles. And while many athletes and coaches may read this right now and cringe (because what competitor loves to lose the outcome?), the intangibles build a stronger human being in the end.

I just finished up two weeks of summer camp last Thursday. The first week, we were at Avon Grove Little League fields, the second at Limerick Community Park. The kids both weeks were great. Something stuck out to me particularly the first week. With no prodding, they cheered each other on during our Softball Olympics day. They were split into two teams, and they started to cheer for each other. Even on different teams. I was taken aback at first, wondering what was going on. I listened carefully as they applauded the other team's efforts, telling each other that they did a good job at that event and even if they didn't win it, they congratulated the person who did. WOW. This was fun to watch. It was very competitive. The Olympic day always is. However, we encourage spirit points. They came dressed in crazy outfits and capes to show their team unity. The second week, they did the same thing.

I started to wonder what this "sportsmanship" thing was all about. How you could honestly be happy for the other team when they won? I watched them have fun, and keep reminding each other that the fun is why there were there. That it's not just about winning. Then I remembered sharing the word "Compete" with them. Compete comes from the Latin *competere*: "To strive WITH or Together." I explained that most of us think that it is about playing AGAINST the other team, not WITH them. But they clearly understood that – at least for them – to compete meant to strive to win WITH the other competitors. In this case, win or lose, they all did it gracefully and with respect and love for the game. And at the end of the day, win or lose, I know they were building stronger human beings throughout the process.

As with most of my stories, I can't help but think of my mom here as well. There isn't much she isn't losing. Her ability to communicate is almost completely gone. She can get out a word here or there, but for the most part we are left with assuming we know what she is trying to tell us with her actions, her eyes, and her smile. She makes noises, and most of the time we can tell if she is unhappy. She is very much aware it, seems; she just can't let us know that. It's a journey for sure, one that I wouldn't jump on if I didn't have to. Yet through it all, it is teaching me so much. Grace is one of those lessons.

My dad told me last week that when he went to feed her dinner the evening that I was there at lunchtime, he asked who came to visit her that day. She said matter-of-factly, "JEN"… Of course, that brought tears to my eyes, as it did to my father as he told me the story. While we are losing pieces of her as time goes by, her grace and dignity are still there in my eyes. When I look at her - with her nails done and her pretty outfits on - she is as beautiful as always. She has lost a lot. We all have, watching this disease continue to take her away from us, but she does it gracefully, every day… with love and a sparkle that will never leave her eyes while she is on this earth.

I spent some time alone with her yesterday. I told her about my 4.0 in my master's degree program and how I have my final paper due this weekend for my "capstone" project and then I will be finished and graduate a part of the International Honor Society. Her eyes lit up and she smiled. She understood. I asked her if she was proud of me and she told me yes with her eyes and partial head nod, her noise of approval. I told her I loved her and she said "I" … and moaned the rest. I know exactly what she meant. I answered with "I know you love me too."

Grace is a way of life. When we do things we don't often like to do or want to do, we find ways to do them with grace, to preserve our dignity, to persevere with heart. We say I'm sorry when we hurt someone, we admit when we are wrong. We are graceful in how we approach sensitive topics. We win, we lose. We do it with class.

It's an art. And sometimes a lost one at that. I am acknowledging the journey and looking for the stronger human being in the end...

And praying for grace in the process.

Chapter 19

It's so beautiful up here...

These last few weeks have had me in various airports, flying to various cities… One thing that I don't really enjoy is flying. I am not afraid of heights, or anything like that… it's more of a space issue. I am not a small person, and fitting in those upright little squares of room is just not comfortable for me. So I don't love to fly. I fly alone most of the time I do fly, and I take my favorite magazines with me so I can catch up on them… Inc., Fast Company, and Entrepreneur seem to be the three I subscribe to that I love to read cover to cover. And, of course, there is always a book or two in my bag when I am finished with the magazines. As a music lover, I also always have my iPod on.

I was on my way from Nashville to Orlando last week, and I was seated next to a mother and her six-year-old little boy, Oliver. He was adorable, as all kids that age tend to be. But one thing stood out to me… his eyes. He was nervous perhaps, but not scared. He looked like he had done this before. His mom took her spot at the window, with Oliver in the middle seat. I always like the aisle to stretch my legs. I had sat before them, so once they got situated, I refastened my seat belt and put my iPod back on. A few minutes later, as we were getting ready to take off, I felt a small hand trying to find its spot on the armrest. It was Oliver's. I moved slightly and gave him room to share with me. He did. A few more minutes, and we were in the air.

It was an early flight (6 a.m.), my favorite time to be in the air. Watching the sunrise as we fly above it is one of the most amazing things I have ever seen. As I took out my magazine and was about to put my iPod back on (yes, the captain just announced that we could use all portable electronic devices...), I heard a husky, little voice, in the most breathtaking of emotions... "It's so beautiful up here."

Right then, I counted quickly... Yep... Five Words. Those were my five words for that day. Oliver had affected me deeply, and he had no idea. His hand was resting on my arm ... for comfort perhaps, or just a place to rest his hand. And as he fell asleep with head nodding motions, his bobbing head even found my shoulder. His mother looked over and very apologetically was about to wake him up to move him... I quickly mouthed to her, NO... he's fine. We both smiled and went back to reading.

One thing was true that flight ...I thought more about the beauty in things than I had in a while. I needed that.

Yes, Oliver... It's so beautiful up here.

It's the process not the outcome that matters.

Enjoy the flight.

Chapter 20

Don't Settle for Less Than...

I was young once. Some days it feels like a long time ago. Others… like it was yesterday. My view of the world seemed small. Yet I often felt like there was so much out there to accomplish and so much I could do.

I remember a conversation that took place once in my kitchen. It was after dinner, and I was probably a freshman in high school. We had just started to clean up, and Jeopardy was on TV. We played every night, my mom, my dad and me. Mom got the ceramic match stick holder off of the stove to keep score. If you got the question right, you got a matchstick to keep track. I did well that night, beating them both. This wasn't normal, as both Dad and Mom were pretty smart at that game most nights.

For some reason, I can clearly remember Mom talking about my history grade that night. I had a big test the next day, and she was telling me to go study right when Jeopardy was over. I sat there hoping for it to be extra long that night, or to find something else to do, to clear the table, help with the dishes… anything so I didn't have to go study. I hated that class: Hammurabi and his code, Hammurabi was the Babylonian King from 1700 B.C. who wrote one of the first lengthy writings in the world. It's funny that I still remember that all this time later. I guess it just stuck in my mind. But at the time, I really didn't care about him or what he had to say.

What Mom said that night hit me, though. It may not have then, but it really does now. When I was asking her why she was on me about studying, she simply said: "Don't settle for less than what you deserve. That goes for anything in your life. But right now, this grade… You should do well on this test because you can. You can study and you can get the grade you want. Don't settle."

I think I could probably quote that word for word all these years later. I got up from the table and found my way to my room, my books sitting on my bed. I sat and opened them. In that notebook, on the inside of the front cover, I wrote… "Don't settle for less than I deserve." I flipped to the section and started to study the stuff I really wasn't interested in. Mom knew this was a hard class. It was Honors Ancient History with a very tough teacher. He didn't settle for less than a student's best. I knew I couldn't either. The next day, I got up and I could hear my mom's voice in my head all the way to school. "Don't settle."

I still hear that voice, all these years later, even when I can't physically hear her voice now. I hear it in my head. "Don't settle for less than what you deserve." I want to live by that, but so often it's hard. We question what it is that we deserve. We get it confused. The young girl who was quiet and shy often doesn't think she deserves more than she has or wonders if this is all she will ever need. At some point, someone has said these words to us all, and at some point we have all questioned what the answer to the riddle really is. What do I deserve? What does that really even mean? Have I done enough to get what I have? Have I done too much and not gotten what I deserve? I have resigned myself to just doing. But maybe I am learning more and more that I would rather figure out how to be instead of do. To be thankful and of gratitude for the life I do have. But to always remain hungry. Never satisfied with mediocrity. Mom wouldn't buy that. But it never really mattered what the answer was. All that mattered, I think, is that we did the job, or put in the work. We would get what we deserve in the end.

I got an A- on that History test. It was like pulling teeth that night to stay up and study everything I needed to remember. I learned a lot more than Hammurabi's Code of laws in the process. I learned that I get out of something what I put in to it. In one night of Jeopardy, I learned more than I did from all the questions and answers for which I had earned matchsticks.

And maybe it was enough. Maybe even though some days that little undeserving girl still comes through, I understand what she was saying. Don't settle for less than...

You can fill in the rest. And when you get it right ... don't forget to get your matchstick.

We're keeping score.

Chapter 21

I'm closer today than yesterday

So there I was, the last leg of the relay team, just about to blow the times we previously set out of the water. I can see the third sprinter coming around the turn. My heart started to race. The adrenaline was flowing freely through my veins. I was so ready to have the fastest time of my life in the 4x100 relay. My teammates built a substantial lead. We were right where we needed to be, now all I needed to do was bring us home. Around the turn she came. I started to move, proper form, hand out and wide open, ready to receive the baton. Clean pass, no contact, I was off. I felt great. I could see out of the corner of my eye the rest of my team coming across the field screaming, jumping up and down as they were running. This was in the bag. We would take the gold medal.

And right then, as if the hundreds of fans surrounding the track could have heard as loudly as I did, A gun shot. Right to my groin. Pop. Pop. My right leg felt like it was five meters behind me, dragging along, trying to keep up. After about three more steps the pain took over and I started to hobble. I was three quarters of the way there. But the finish line could have been a mile away for all I knew. The pain was unreal. I heard the gasps around me. All in a few steps. Pain. Noise. Gasps. I was going down. But not before I threw my body over the line.

I just. Have. To. Get. There.

It was the only thought that consumed my mind as I watched the team to the right of me fly by me, then the left. Just need to finish. If we don't finish, we don't move on.

Finish. The. Damn. Race.

It's all I could muster up. I saw the trainer and coaches all pile around the finish line as I came hurdling across in such a non-graceful fashion, literally collapsing as I did. Groin muscle. Need I say more?

That would be the last time I ran track.

I think of that moment in eighth grade when I could fly. I was fast. I was strong. I was voted by my peers in our yearbook that year as most athletic girl. But I was hiding. Most people knew of me as the athlete. I managed to get good grades, took accelerated classes, honors and was in the gifted and talented program in the school system my whole life. But did they really know ME? Did I, for that matter? Really know ME? WOW, there was so much more. I was an insecure kid. Quiet, shy, afraid I wouldn't fit in. Funny, I think we all have moments of that awkward eighth grader in our lives at some point, even when we are 37. Perhaps even when we are 67.

However, what I have found is so much better than that scared, imperfect little kid. Every day we stretch ourselves, every day we push our limits, every day we find new ways to be ourselves. We thrive. In so many ways, so many opportunities, we get better. And we realize quickly that regardless of what we accomplish, we are that much wiser, that much older and that much more able to understand each other.

And the truth is, that is what's most important anyway. That quiet scared kid... the one who everyone thought was confident all her life? Yeah, she's still here every once in a while. I love that though. I will never forget where I came from. But for where I am going?

Let's just say I'm closer today than yesterday.

Chapter 22

Shine with all your light.

Sometimes the moon keeps me up at night. Or maybe it's just my heavy brain working overtime, and I like to blame it on the moon. It's so bright tonight, racing through my curtains, falling right across my face, as I lay buried under my covers in the cold winter chill that seeps through the old windowpanes of my bedroom. The moon acts like it needs to get in because it has something important to tell me. I spend extra time these nights by the door as the dogs are outside, amazed at how the night sky lights up like the dawn. It's 1:16 a.m., and it's one of those nights.

Bright like the dawn.

Or maybe my mind just won't turn off, as usual. Wanting to sleep but filled with so much thought. Sometimes I see or hear something during the day that won't let me go. I am my father's daughter. Awake, thinking, feeling.

I watched a story of a family on the news tonight that lost their house last week in a fire. All of their belongings were just gone. I often wonder what that must feel like, losing everything to something you can't control. Another family's car was broken into while the father was having surgery for cancer. Their son had paid a high price in Iraq, almost dying in combat. His health and way of life will forever be affected. Their Christmas gifts were stolen from the car, the window shattered. They have no money to replace the gifts, only the window to keep out that cold winter chill. I wonder if the moon shines as brightly over their house tonight. And if it doesn't, maybe they could borrow mine. I want to help. I called the news station so I could write down their address in the hope that I could shine even a drop of light their way. To let them know that the hope they are searching for is still there. I will drive there and hand them an envelope tomorrow.

I also think about those people whom I have lost along the way, those people who have made me who I am. Perhaps they have something to do with the moon. Perhaps THEY are the reason it shines so brightly just when I need it to most.

I question the moon tonight. I ask it to give more light. Maybe it's just not enough. There are people out there who need it. People who are searching for any light at all…Hard times, uncertain futures, love lost, sickness, fear, loneliness.

Maybe if I could shine as brightly, I could help the moon. In some strange way, I think we all do. We all give an energy that shines for those around us. And maybe, right when they need it most.

Some days, we could be the one to change a life. We may never know it. But we keep shining.

In the little things we do, we could give someone hope in a moment we may not even understand.

Giving that light away seems like the only logical thing to do then.

I choose to reflect the moon. I choose to give what I am given.

So go ahead, moon, shine with all your light.

I can close my eyes now.

It was dark, the sun had just faded into the trees and the moon was just a sliver in the autumn sky. She looked up with a sense of wonder.

It was so big. And the sky seemed so far away.

And in that moment, she felt so incredibly small.

And scared.

And lost.

Her long, drawn out breath continued to feel labored.

Climbing that steep hill was about all she had left in her.

"There you are."

He rose to greet her.

"I made it," her only reply as she slowly walked by him without an acknowledgement.

Emotionless and still.

She stared over the peak of the hill down onto the valley below.

Wondering what she left behind and who she was supposed to be.

She continued to look down.

"WOW, it's so amazingly beautiful up here, isn't it?"

She forgot he was there.

All she could see was what she just came from.

And the longer she looked, the more she felt lost.

He asked again...

"This view is incredible, don't you think?"

A tear fell slowly. Then another.

She wept openly at all she left behind.

"You cry because of what you lost and who you should have been," he said. "I know. I have lived it."

"But if you would just turn this way, and look up... you will see the beauty of all there is to become."

The last tear hit her scuffed up black boot with a vengeance.

Chapter 23

I'm not lucky... just blessed.

Today is Tuesday, the day I usually go visit Mom. My aunt comes to feed her lunch on Tuesdays and my sister came to town this week to visit as well. Today was Tuesday. But it wasn't like any other Tuesday for some reason. Something happened for me today that I am not so sure I can explain. Something in me today saw things differently. Mom was good today. She laughed at our jokes, listened to our conversation. And when I left her, I kissed her on the cheek as I always do and told her I love her. She responded. Not in words, but in sounds. I know she was saying she loves me too.

Mom had a roommate for a while in the beginning before she got her own room down the hall about a month ago. This lady is a very petite little bit of a thing who still can walk, zipping around on her walker that doubles as a seat when she feels like sitting down.

Eleanor is the nicest little old lady I think I have met in a very long time. She just adores Mom and always comes to check on her now that they are not living in the same room anymore. Today, she saw us all in her new room feeding Mom her lunch, and she popped in to say hi. She told us stories of her weekend with her family. Eleanor is lucky; she is able to leave the home for holidays and spend time with her children for a cookout at their house. She told us how great the weekend was and of her double Manhattans that had her feeling fine. She had us laughing. She even had my mom laughing.

We can tell my mom knows Eleanor's sweet little voice. It was when she was turning to leave that I had a moment that has lingered with me all day. I don't remember who said it, but someone asked her if it's hard to come back there after spending time with her family. She said it was and that she has been there too long, even though it's only been seven months. Then she quickly took away any feelings of sadness or sorry by saying this: "I'm not lucky... just blessed."

I smiled. Immediately counting on my fingers the five words she just threw at us and walked away. What did that mean? I didn't really get it until my sister shared a story of cute little 95-year-old Eleanor's life. You see, she actually was praying about a year ago for God to take her,that she was done and just wanted to die. And then... she changed her mind. And as she puts it... now, she is actually living. She is enjoying every day, making friends in the nursing home, enjoying the time she has with family and her new friends. She blew my mom a kiss when she was leaving and said twice, "Oh, bless her heart, she's laughing." She's 95 years old, with a mass growing inside. But Eleanor is blessed.

I left there today experiencing a deep feeling that I couldn't explain. I came home and just sat on my couch for a little bit unsure of what to do next. I felt like I had a lot to do, but wasn't sure why I felt drained. Or maybe even a little bit melancholy. I was feeling; that's why. Feeling things about life and death and questioning all of it. I get deep sometimes, wondering about my purpose in life, about my own existence... asking if I am fulfilling my calling in the best way that I know how. I often ask questions to the universe, to God, asking what more I can do. And then it hit me again, an opportunity that I missed that I still can't get out of my mind.

I was driving home from New Jersey the other day and passed a woman probably my age in a minivan that looked like it just got sideswiped. The side mirror was dangling and there were big scrapes along the side of the van. She looked to be crying on the phone, shaken up. No other car was around, so I would assume it was a hit and run. I tried to get over off the ramp where she was but cars were flying right behind me. I couldn't stop or I would have gotten run into myself. I wonder how often in life that happens and we don't even know it. We don't stop even when we see something around us that is going on. Or, how often we "pass" things in our lives that we don't even see and therefore could do nothing about. I can't get that woman off my mind. I wanted to stop and help, but I wasn't able to. It still bothers me four days later. I don't even know what I could have done to help, but perhaps it was a moment of just letting her know she was not alone.

I recorded Oprah's last show last week and picked tonight, for some reason, to watch it. It was always my desire to go to see her show live. On my "127 Things to do before I die list," I actually wrote, "Be invited on Oprah with my book." I think there was a small piece of me as I watched this last show tonight that saw that dream die. I know that is no longer an option. It was weird how that actually was a sad moment for me. But the show itself moved me in ways I cannot explain. I feel shaken. Not in a bad way, but in a way that almost felt like an awakening. So much of what I have pursued so far in my life has come from little moments of inspiration here and there from the people I respect most. She is high up on that list, and honestly, like the Oprah show or not, she has done some amazing things for this world and the people in it. And her challenge for all of us has always been to live the life we were called to live... and to be thankful in that blessing.

Her last show was extremely moving. It was my reminder today of why I was feeling the way I was. She said that we are here "To live from the heart of yourself, knowing what sparks the light in you, so you, in your own way, can illuminate the world." I am very thankful that I watched that show tonight… Three times.

"Everybody has a calling… DO not get it confused. It doesn't have to be something… that makes you famous… You carry whatever you're supposed to be doing, carry that forward and don't waste anymore time… Use your life to serve the world… Your being alive makes worthiness your birthright. You alone are enough."

I can't tell you how many times I rewound and listened to those words tonight. Thinking about Eleanor wanting God to take her …I wonder how often my mom thinks and feels the same. She just can't tell us that. I think about all the times that those around us are suffering, often quietly… Often alone. Feeling incomplete and empty, ashamed and unworthy. I have felt all of those things, too. Some days I still do. We all DO just want to be validated. We all just want to be HEARD. What a lesson today. What a feeling of gratitude I have for feeling. I so much want to make it my calling to listen to those around me so they know what they say matters.

I heard these words on pause and rewind. Letting them sink in. They hit me hard. I watch my mom in her chair, not able to communicate almost at all. I watch Eleanor get around great, sharp as a tack at the age of 95. I watch a woman on TV share with the world, 30,000 guests, thousands of shows, those simple words I wrote above. Yes, Oprah… everyone has a calling. Everyone has a purpose. And sometimes gratitude, reaching out to help others, understanding our common connection, just our need to be heard and validated is what our calling is. And maybe some days I am not so lucky.

Maybe some days I don't bring the best energy to myself. But just like 95-year-old Eleanor, I am blessed. And I am willing to take responsibility for my own energy. And I am not waiting for anyone to fix me, inspire me, or complete me. I am all of those things. Thank you to the three women who reminded me of that today.

I'm not lucky... just blessed.

Chapter 24

There's a beauty in resilience.

I walked into the lobby of Berks Heim as mom napped, on my way out after feeding her lunch. She wasn't awake for long, so I figured there was no reason to sit and watch her sleep some more. And on my way out, in the lobby, I noticed what I always noticed. There they were, as always, on the couch in the front foyer of the main entrance. Like on prom night, cuddled up together in each other's arms, gazing into each other's eyes, was a husband and wife spending every moment together in some amazingly real love cocoon.

Every time I leave, they are there, holding each other. Just sitting, staring in the same direction. I smiled at them today as I always do. The older gentleman smiled back and said hello. "How are you today?" I inquired. "Oh, just fine," he smiled back as I walked past. One of them lives there from what I can tell. The other comes to visit daily and they spend their time pinned together on that couch. Like they own it. Like no one else could do it justice. I doubt anyone could. I smiled and fought back a tear as I walked out to the crisp, cool March afternoon.

The love they have between them is an amazing picture of beauty, of being at the end of life and holding on to what is perfect. Resilience isn't in everyone's vocabulary. Some people find the breakdown easier than the rebuild. There seems to be solace sometimes in the letting go, the falling apart… the excuses and reasons to just give up in that moment. We all have them; we all do it. It is human nature to feel sorry for ourselves sometimes. And those moments are probably just as important so we can thrive in the triumph over adversity, in the beauty of turning the bad to good.

My softball team has had its fair share of adversity, of the hard and the bad…of the loss and the injury, on and off the field. And through it all, I have watched some amazing things happen. What excites me the most is the fact that there is solace and peace even in losing. And I am not even talking about on the field. We have gone through so much off the field, in our every day lives, that I realize softball is secondary to what is happening here.

Life is unfolding in ways that sometimes we just don't even understand. We fall down. We get up. We find the courage to do it all over again, regardless of how many times it takes, how many scrapes and burns we tend to. We build stronger bonds. We find ties that we can't unravel. We hold the rope. For each other and ourselves. We make the mistakes count. And we stop counting the mistakes. We fall down. Again. We get up. Again. And through it all, we find a beauty we can't match in anything else we do. We look for it, but we just don't see it in others. The times of real gentleness are the ones we grab hold of. We don't let go. We, too, wrap our arms around each other and smile. We are more than "just fine" today. We bounce back, stronger, better, and with more love in our hearts than before. We welcome it. We don't back down when the fire gets hot.

We hold the rope.
We hold the rope.
We hold the rope.
There's a beauty in resilience.

Chapter 25

Let the mind transcend limitations

I learned how to walk when I was young, younger than usual.
Mom told me I fell a lot. But I walked early because of all the
times I fell. I think about that sometimes, wondering what it
would be like if we all learned to walk as adults. I have a feeling
we never would. We would be afraid of falling, or bruising a
knee, or cracking our head open.

We would hold back. Not because we knew better, but because
we were afraid.

Afraid of being told we can't, afraid of failing, afraid of success.
Afraid that we are the ones who are telling ourselves we can't.
Afraid of fear.

We put limits on ourselves as we get older. The older we get,
the more limits. I can't do that... I am too old, or short, or
overweight, or not smart enough, or not fast enough, or strong
enough. I will never be able to be this or that, or I know I will
never do the things I want because I am too this or too that. And
it goes on and on. We tell ourselves stories and make excuses.
We put limits in places where they don't belong.

Last week I was at the gym and my trainer put some weight on the leg press. I didn't ask, I didn't really care. I just did what I was supposed to do.

She told me… 6 reps at 260 pounds. She raised the weight for the second set. Again, I didn't ask. I assumed it was just a little more. Five reps this time. No sweat.

I started to push the weight up. It barely moved. I thought I was just tired.

"Come on, push, Jen." She kept on me. I knew I had to lift it. I had no reason not to.

I pushed. One.

Tapped down and pushed back up. Two. It felt surprisingly heavy. Wow, I am dragging today. I must be really spent.

Tap. Three.

"Push it out; come on. Keep those knees straight."

Katie barked out my motivation as I tapped again. Four.

Come on. One more.

I finally got through the last one.

"And relax," she said.

Wow. My legs were shaking. But again, I thought nothing of it. Just another tough set. One minute; then I do it again.

I looked to my right, to where the weights were. I looked down. I looked down again.

"Wait…What did you say the number was I was lifting?"

She looked on my chart to double check.

"260… why?"

"Ummm, that says 360!"

She looked at the weight stack, then at me. "Oops," she chuckled as I started to laugh. "Are you serious? If you had told me I was lifting 360 pounds, I would have told you that you were crazy."

I would have said I couldn't. I would have had 17 different excuses why I couldn't.

I did it because I didn't know any better.

Last season, on February 1st, the Ursinus College softball team did one pushup at the end of practice. They looked at me like I was crazy when I had them end practice with just one pushup.

On February 2, we did two. On February 3, three. Every day, we added one more.

On May 5, we ended our season with 67 pushups.

If I had told my girls they would be doing 67 pushups at once, they would have told me they couldn't do that. They would have had their own 17 different excuses why they couldn't.

The limits we put on ourselves create the barriers that we often use as our comfy pillow for a bad night's sleep. We find times that we curl up with our excuses instead of kicking them out of bed. We allow them to dictate what we dream about and how rested we feel.

We are afraid. We hate to fail.

Yet, I would have never known how far I could go if I had never tried.

Perhaps this is the day we will allow the excuses to fall away.

Perhaps this is the day we will make a choice to learn how to walk again, regardless of how many times we fall down.

Today...

Perhaps today is the day we will have no limits.

Chapter 26

Life happens as it will.

It's not easy to watch the news on most nights. Tonight was no different. I watched the updates about the shooting of the Congresswoman in Tucson and about an entire apartment building burning to the ground while the residents stood there, watching it happen. Some people, like congresswoman Giffords' intern, move into immediate action toward the scene. Others go away and get help. And still others are in too much shock to do much of anything.

It is not until tragedy happens in your own sight that you really know how you will respond. I can't say I have witnessed a shooting, but I have been at the scene of accidents, a robbery at gun point, and even a bad sports injury where the victim lost consciousness. I have seen what I do in a crisis situation. I am content with my response.

The truth is, after watching the news tonight, I sat again and contemplated about my own life. I watched those who lost their homes to that fire talk about how they lost everything they had. They had no insurance, no chance of getting them back. In the blink of an eye... it was just gone. And no one can change that. One guy even talked about how he didn't even take the time to grab his wallet because he was too busy worried about finding the cat. So he had no identification, no money, no access to his accounts. Nothing. All he had was a body in jeans and a sweatshirt. That's all he has left of his life. Thankfully, he has that.

No one can explain why these things happen to certain people and why others are the onlookers, rushing to their aid or running to get help or watching in shock feeling helpless. We don't choose these events. They choose us. I talk so much about choice because I believe there is a lot we choose and a lot we can change or affect. But the sad reality is that there are things in life we over which we just don't have any control. They just happen as they will, and we move with them to accommodate. We carry on.

Some days, I wonder when the next "non-choosable" event will happen in my life. I wonder what it will be. I know my mom didn't choose this awful illness any more than she chose to have blue eyes when she was born. My friend didn't choose to have a cancerous brain tumor. My uncle didn't choose his heart disease. And yet, through it all, we choose to laugh anyway, in spite of our non-choosables. It's one of my mom's best qualities.

I remember one day laughing with her while I was visiting. It was a good day. She seemed happy and content. I smiled at her at one point and told her she was silly today. She managed to somewhat understandably infer, "Well, what choice do I really have?" And at that point I realized that even through the "stuff" that life gives us, the "stuff" we don't choose... we have a choice how to react to it. My mom laughs. I can't thank God enough for her ability to do so now because she has very little ability left to do anything else. Regardless of what some may think, I think she navigates well. She grows stronger in my eyes every day. I respect her for that.

I pray hard for that laughter to continue.

I add the Congresswoman and the people who lost their homes to that list tonight.

I remind myself to choose my responses with my heart.

Life happens as it will.

Carry on.

Navigate well.

Pray hard.

Part Four.

Surrender

"I know now that letting go is the only way to hold on." –jlc

And the rain came that day with a vengeance.

*"How do I...? When will it end...? What can I figure out to...?"
The questions seemed insurmountable. They kept coming. Like
the leaks in the roof as the downpour came inside.*

"Lighten the load woman... why don't you just let go?"

"What?" She seemed shocked at his disgraceful comment.

*"That's like not caring... why would I do that?" She barked
back at him.*

"I said let go... Not 'don't care.' That's two different things."

"Sounds very much the same to me."

*She felt dumb engaging in a conversation that she would not be
able to win. Or at least keep up with.*

"He always does this. Puts me in my place," she thought to herself. *"What if he's right?"* She got up to reposition and immediately he called her out.

"Uncomfortable, are we?" he chuckled through his words.

She uncrossed her legs again and put her arm back around the back of the chair.

He was leaning against the desk looking at her the whole time, watching her move around in her seat, as if he knew.

"When you can get comfortable, that's truly when you can let go. We call it surrendering. And it's a good thing. You should try it sometime."

All she could picture was the little white flag waving from under a pile of leaves. Weakness, giving up... not caring.

She needed to change her perspective if she was going to really grasp this.

He knew that.

He reached out to take her hand, gently and lovingly.

"Here, grab on. I will teach you how to let go."

Chapter 27

Homeless. Hungry. I need help.

Life has a way of popping up when you least expect it to... Funny things, tough to handle things, lessons and sadness often appear seemingly out of nowhere. People often surprise us. In both good and bad ways. And sometimes we fight through the bad just to have the moment of good we have longed for. These weeks get busy. But my goal when I open my eyes every day is to find where my energy is to go and give all of it unselfishly. When I stop keeping score, I am truly living from my heart. I have struggled in my life in many ways. I have been fortunate enough to have a strong "network" that will not let me fall.

Last week, I was driving to pick up a client from school for our afternoon together and passed by an older gentleman on the side of the road. He was sitting on the curb with a cardboard sign. So often I see this man – or someone just like him - and I want so badly to help with more than a couple bucks. I have heard people question whether it's true or if people who hold signs on the street for money then go home after a day's work and get a hot shower and have a meal while watching the game. I just don't think that way. If someone asks for help, I want to help.

I had to get to the school by a certain time to pick up my client, so I pulled in and parked, still thinking about the old man on the side of the road. When I finally got to my client, we drove off to our usual pizza spot to chat, and I knew that I would pass that spot where the man was sitting on the way there. When I got close, I told her about the man I saw and that I wanted to see if he was still there. I pulled over the hill and, sure enough, he was sitting on the curb. As I was pulling over, my 11-year-old client reached down into her bag to take out a dollar to share with the old man. I knew I had a 20 in my wallet, so I took that out, and together we gave him our 21 dollars. I asked if he was ok. He smiled and said that he just started receiving food stamps within the past week, "even though you can't tell," he said, as he pointed to his bony body. He was trying to find a place to stay for the night because the rain was coming. He usually stayed with a friend when he could afford it, but his friend was charging him $20 a night to stay there. He smiled and said that he was thankful to us that he would have a place to stay that night. He also excitedly told us that he just started working at a pizza shop so that will help him afford food and a roof over his head. He thanked us again, and then said "God Bless you."

His sign read "Homeless. Hungry. I need help." I thought about the sign as I drove off. We talked about it, and it became a great life lesson moment for me to discuss with my 11-year-old client. We went on about our day, but something about that man stuck in my head. His simple sign, asking for help, written in faded black marker on a tattered cardboard flap, had really gotten my attention. Maybe it was a SIGN that I was supposed to see that day.

"I need help" is a courageous phrase, not only to say it, but to write it down in permanent marker.

I drove home in silence, still thinking about the man and the sign. Thinking about his courage and his smile. Wishing sometimes that I had a faded black marker and a tattered cardboard flap. Maybe not to write those same words, but to ask for help, to ask for understanding and love, to ask for forgiveness from family and friends. To just handwrite it, whatever it is, so it wouldn't be perfect.

We so often take for granted the things in our lives that have been there, the people who have supported us, the fact that we will be able to make it right tomorrow if we just don't feel like it today. Sometimes we need to hold up our cardboard sign and hope the people around us can or are willing to read it. Maybe one of my biggest faults is that I have gone through life asking how I can help others more often than how they may be able to help me. Maybe I didn't give them enough of a chance to be that person in my life.

I still can see the cardboard. I wonder if it made it through the last rain, or if the writing smudged.

The irony of a permanent marker may just be too much for me.

Chapter 28

Learning not to hate different.

It's a whole new year. So much is still the same. So much is different. I am learning to adjust as my life shifts. I used to think I needed to stand on the rock and let the world adjust around me. Now, I understand it doesn't really work that way. I need to work on being more pliable, more flexible.

I have been reading the Tao Te Ching (a classic book written around the sixth century BC) again, and while I love to learn about spirituality and religion, I don't claim to understand all such thoughts and beliefs. However, I am intrigued by a lot of what the Tao explores.

In the Tao, the author, Lao Tzu, says that when you are born, you are pliable and flexible and when you die you are hard and rigid. And in the process of growing older in between, we change states often. We grow less flexible with change; we learn to be set in our ways.

I am working really hard to reverse that inflexibility in my own life. But habits are hard to break. Change is hard to accept. So, I don't like to look at it as change. Instead, I look at it as different.

I had a conversation about this concept the other day with a close friend. She asked, "What's the difference between change and different then?" I replied, "Good question." I sat and thought about it for a bit and realized that my own definition or rather distinction is this: Change requires action. Different is just a description. It just... is. I feel there is a lot in my life lately that just... is - neither good nor bad; just different.

I have had many people ask me this past week how the holidays were a standard question this time of year. I keep answering the same. "Different." This is the first year that my mom wasn't at home with us. But I have to say I felt a love in my family this year that was heightened because of it. So it wasn't a good feeling not having her there, but it wasn't as bad as I guess it could have been because of the love that I felt that day.

The holiday season often brings up many childhood memories. One of my favorite memories from growing up was our New Year's Eve ritual as a family. We often spent the whole evening together. Most of my friends would be getting together and I was home with my parents and most of my siblings and their families. We spent all of our holidays together. We didn't know anything else. At midnight, we would share champagne, hug and kiss each other (which in a family as big as mine often took quite a few minutes), and then carry on with the snacks and drinks until close to 2 a.m. The part I loved the most was going outside just after the hugs and kisses subsided with mom and her pots and pans. I LOVED to make a lot of noise as a kid, and standing on the front steps of the house, as many of us as possible, we would bang the pots and pans as a fun ritual to signal the start of the New Year. Mom always says it was good luck, to keep the evil spirits away from the new beginning. I just liked doing it because I was allowed to make noise that late at night.

To this day, I still go outside with a pot and a wooden spoon just after midnight and I bang the heck out of the pot, just for a couple seconds. I do it because it makes me feel closer to Mom.

This was the first year I wasn't able to call and hear her voice at midnight. So making a loud noise on my front steps I guess was my way of wishing her Happy New Year from here. It's still the same tradition. Even though I am on different steps with different pots and my mom isn't by my side. It's different, but it's very much the same.

Starting a new year is sometimes a daunting task. We are often so bombarded by the questions and the ads on TV about what our New Year's Resolutions are. We feel we need to have them. We need to satisfy a tradition. Or we need to make ourselves feel like we are going to change something we don't like about ourselves. This year, I didn't make any resolutions. I just didn't. I made a decision that I am going to just start living the way I want to live every day instead of waiting for January 1st, which only comes once a year on my calendar. I always have goals. I believe in making manageable objectives, or "intentions." But instead of beating myself up for the "I'm going to lose weight," or "I'm going to make more money," or "I'm going to spend more time with my family" resolutions that grace most of our lists, or maybe the "I'm going to finish the project I started" or "I'm going to go back to school" or whatever other resolutions I could have made, … - you get my point.

Too often, we wait for things to be perfect before we start something, or we wait for the right time to work on what we "should" be doing all along. So much of life is outside of our control. It just… is.
This year, I choose to take "different" head-on.
And I have decided that I don't hate it.

Chapter 29

And I did Play Pool.

I turned down playing pool more than once in my life. Grandma C. had a table in her basement that always lured me when we visited once or twice a year. There were usually not many kids my age to play with, so I often ventured down there alone, possibly with a cousin or two I didn't really know. I was young, maybe 10 or 11. Too cool to hang with mom and dad, but not cool enough to hang with my older brother or cousins. SO, off to the basement I would go, pick up the pool stick and shoot the balls around. I never really knew how to play. No one ever really taught me.

I was 21 and in a local bar with some friends. We went to that specific hang out because it had a few nice pool tables. There I was, standing against the wall, a comfortable spectator. I was in a club when I was in my mid-twenties and felt bad because my date wanted to play pool and I, of course, didn't. I have been asked so many times by so many people in my life and each time, I found a reason not to play. I call them reasons, but I guess they're really excuses.

The funny thing is, it's not that I hated the idea. I just didn't know if I would be good at it. So I just wouldn't try. Not in front of people, anyway. When I was 11, it wouldn't have been a big deal. I wasn't supposed to know how to shoot pool. But by the age of 25, you would think I would have figured it out. I didn't want to not succeed. Period.

Ahhhh, sweet perfectionism. Self-admittedly, one of my best qualities, and at the same time one of the simple things that has held me back so many times in my life. I know I am not alone in that. Often, the athletes I work with sit in the chair across from my desk in my office and talk about how they beat themselves up if they walk a batter, or allow a goal to score, or just not get it right. One time can send us freefalling into negative self-talk. We say some amazing things to ourselves when no one is listening. The problem? WE ARE listening... and in that case, we continue to tell ourselves we aren't good enough or we can't do something. No one else may even know. But we do, and that's all that matters.

So I hid the fact that I was afraid to play pool because I was afraid of being bad at something I didn't know how to do. I just told people I didn't like to play. How silly...it's pool. Really not a big deal, right? Well, for me it was. Fear can be paralyzing. And I am writing about it because it's my story. It affected me more than I knew.

Until a Saturday afternoon at a friend's house not so long ago for a graduation party. I have a wonderful friend who has an amazing way of reminding me of the simple joys in life. Anyone who knows Ryan Garrity knows her amazing heart and the beauty she sees in the simple things. She was at the party too with her parents and older sister and wanted nothing more than to play pool with me. Finally, I couldn't say no any longer. I knew she would be horribly disappointed if I didn't play.

I picked up a stick with a few other people around and knew it was time. Of course, it was the most fun I had had in a long time. Ryan took away my need to do it perfectly, and reminded me just sharing that time with her that she still talks about to this day was a simple joy. Pool was just the vehicle. I was excited to have overcome a hurdle. Little did she know that day, she actually helped me get past one of my fears. It wasn't about pool at all, it was about me not wanting to fail. Yeah, I hit some bad shots, but also actually had some good ones. It was kind of fun... and I found out that I wasn't so bad at it after all.

I am still a "recovering perfectionist"... it's like a disease. But I laugh at myself a lot more now, and I am not afraid to fail. I know that if I fall flat on my face, I am 5 feet 11 inches closer to where I wanted to go. I get up, and I keep moving, one foot in front of the other.

I learned what a "scratch" is, and I know, metaphorically speaking, I have done that a hundred times in my life. So you take the penalty and you keep moving. I feel like I have gotten past a lot of the negative parts that perfectionism can carry. I have accepted my failures and always vow to learn from them. It's kind of fun to laugh at yourself when you make mistakes. I have learned a lot about myself that way. I am proud of those accomplishments... I got over a lot of hurdles.

And I did play pool...

Chapter 30

Cleanup is a Woman's Job.

It was 1991. I was a freshman at the University of Delaware. Colleen Webster was my E-110 teacher. E-110 is a Freshman English class that all first year students must take. I actually entered my first semester as a psychology major. I was ready to take on and fix the world. And then I met Colleen Webster. She was a graduate assistant professor finishing her doctorate at UD, teaching Freshman English. She was one of the best teachers I have ever had. I respected her so much for the way she taught, the way she allowed us to creatively write and express ourselves, the way she taught us to see things from every perspective; how the written word can be so powerful.

Toward the end of the semester, Colleen asked me to stay after class one day to talk to her. I was nervous. SHE wants to talk to ME? Either I did something wrong, or she really likes my work as much as she tells me she does. I will never forget that day. Because the next morning, I walked over to the Administration office to change my major to English. She told me I should be writing, that anything else would be a waste of my talent. I believed her. Or, more importantly, she believed in me.

Sometimes, I have learned along the way, that it takes only one. One person to believe in you, one person to reach out and motivate you to be something more than you thought possible. One moment that changes a life.

One of my last essays that semester was to be about a time when you were younger and you accomplished something that you never thought you could. My essay was titled "Cleanup is a woman's job." I remember her face when I handed it in. She looked puzzled, almost surprised coming from a liberal female with a social voice like my writing portrayed. I smiled at her and walked away. I figured I would let her read it for herself.

I was seven when my dad and I walked into the Tenafly Public Library for Little League signups. Back then, there was no softball for girls my age. Softball started in sixth grade. If I wanted to play ball, it would have to be baseball with the boys. I didn't think twice about it when we walked in to put my name down and pay my fee. My dad didn't either. He was always very supportive of me and always told me I could do anything a boy could do as an athlete. I believed him. And more importantly, I knew he believed in me. A few weeks later, the season would start.

I can still remember pulling into the parking lot at the field downtown that first time, sitting in the car, looking across the way at all the boys gathering on the field. My dad looked at me and smiled. "Are you sure you want to do this?" he asked. "You can always back out if you don't feel like it's for you, or you feel uncomfortable at any time." I looked at him, then across the field. I remember opening the door to get out and not saying a word. My dad followed my lead. I got my bat and my glove out of the trunk of our light blue Buick Century. The trunk lid squeaked as it closed. I started the long walk across to the other field, my dad in tow. I was quiet, shy and a little bit awkward in situations that I was unsure of. But something made me walk over there. I saw a couple boys I went to school with and felt a little better. They were on my team. That would hopefully be ok.

As the first few weeks of the season wore on, my dad started to help out as an assistant coach. I loved it. I started to play better every week, and by mid season, I decided I wanted to try catching. My dad was a little worried, as this was probably the most dangerous spot on the field for a girl to play. I convinced him to let me try. I put on all the gear and with my long pony tail sticking out the back of the helmet, and the little rosebuds on my underpants that you could see through the light grey baseball pants, I made my way behind home plate.

That year, I hit my first homerun. I made All Stars. I batted cleanup. I was one of the best players on my team... and I was a girl. At first, the boys didn't know whether to slide into me, run me over, or avoid hurting me at home. I wasn't afraid. Not for a minute. I just wanted to play.

One game, at the end of the season, a young umpire showed up right before game time. It was his first season. We went out for the first inning, me in my armor walking to the plate, when the umpire stopped me before I started warming up the pitcher.

"Excuse me... Are you wearing a cup?" The kid in blue was dead serious. I looked at him confused and answered... "Ummm No." He then proceeded to tell me that I needed to wear a cup. I thought he was joking and ignored him for a second. My dad came walking out sensing there was an issue. The umpire then turned to him and said "If she wants to catch, she needs a cup." He chuckled and told the umpire he couldn't be serious and was about to walk away when the umpire responded. "It says in the rule book that all catchers must wear a protective cup. If she wants to catch, she needs to wear a cup."

At that, I stormed over to the equipment bag and dug through it until I found what I imagined was a cup. I picked it up, shoved it into my pants and walked back to the plate. "There," I said, "Are you happy? I am wearing a cup. Let's play ball."

My dad was trying to get me to come out and he told me that he would put someone else in, but I refused. Besides it being a tad bit uncomfortable, I wore the cup because I just wanted to play ball. I didn't care that I was the only girl on the team. I didn't care that I had to wear a cup to catch. I just wanted to play.

My parents often told me stories of when I was five years old, of how I would sit on my great-grandmother's back porch with her on her green metal sofa and listen to a whole Phillies' game on the radio. We would both stare off into the back yard and just listen. She would live to be 100. No one was a bigger Phillies fan than my great-grandmother, Annie Palmer.

But the real story in my parents' eyes is how a five-year-old kid could sit still for that long and LISTEN to a baseball game on a radio with a little old lady who could barely hear. My love of the game would never be challenged. I played for one reason: "For Love of the Game." I didn't realize then how much those five words would mean to me later in my life.

I played with all my heart. Every day; every game. I took it seriously. And I proved to all the boys in town, the coaches, and even the umpires that cleanup absolutely is a woman's job.

Even Colleen Webster had to agree.

Chapter 31

Living this day without excuses.

I've known a seven-year-old with only one foot. A mother, blind and unable to see the beauty in her newborn's face. A man with no limbs who continues to teach the world that it is the soul that is most important. Homeless, no food, no clean clothes, no shoes, perhaps no love. I have seen it. But I don't live it. I have all my limbs, I have a home, food, the ability to walk to my basement whenever I want to wash my clothes. I have love in my life.

Virginia Woolf once said, "Arrange whatever pieces come your way." And often, I can do that. Some days, however, my headache takes over, my neck hurts, my knees ache and I just don't feel like it. Some days, I find every excuse I can to NOT walk downs stairs and wash my clothes or clean the bathrooms or put laundry away. I just don't feel like it is always good enough. Then I think about the man I passed last week on the street in town with all of his belongings in a shopping cart, looking for a warm place to lie down for the night. And I think of how blessed I really am. And I think about who I am, and who he is. And then I realize that perhaps those belongings don't make me who I am, and the lack of them doesn't make him any less than me.

We find ways to forget. Some days, I think we really do. We take for granted what we have and who we have to give us reassurance and love and keep us safe and warm. We don't remember to say thank you for the little things. We assume they will be there. I am really learning how not to do that as my family navigates through the last portion of my mom's life. I am learning how much the little moments mean, how a hand to touch her and eyes to see her are so very important to me now. My awareness is so much richer, so much deeper now. I am thankful to have those simple things in my life when before I would have taken them for granted.

I was 11 when my first nephew Tyler was born. I was the "young, cool" aunt, always just a little older, but not so old that I was far from understanding. Tyler was the one who named my mom "Gummy", we think trying to say Grammy, but just never really getting it right. So "Gummy" would stick, and even to this day I have to smile as I hear all three of those boys, now tall and handsome men in their 20's call my mom "Gummy."

My second nephew, Ryan, who is now 6'5", 24 years old and a basketball coach at his former high school, is one of the nicest guys I know (In fact, they all are... and I'm not just saying it... They truly are amazing young men.)

Ryan couldn't have been more than five or six at the time, when he was playing in the living room in the house I grew up in. My mom had been known to collect antique tea sets. In fact, there was one that we all put money together to buy her for Christmas one year that was hand-painted and signed by the artist. At the time, I didn't really get it, I mean, it was pretty and everything, but it seemed to me a little crazy to spend that kind of money on a tea set. But what did I know? I was a punk just going to college who didn't really care about tea pots and sugar bowls, I guess.

All of a sudden, there was a loud crash. We all went running into the living room, and there, with huge eyes, was Ryan staring at the pieces of a sugar bowl on the table. Big, huge tears started to well up in his eyes. I just knew this wouldn't be good. My sister immediately grabbed his arm, and with that motherly "you are in really big trouble, mister" look, she asked what he did. Right away, without blaming someone else, or saying the dog did it… he just looked up at her, scared to death, and cried. All he could get out was that he was sorry. No excuses. Just that he was sorry. And it seemed sincere. My sister immediately scolded him, saying loudly, "YOU BROKE ONE OF GUMMY's POSSESSIONS!" Ryan replied through his sobbing tears, gasping for air: "I don't even know what a possession is…"

And in that moment, it seemed like all was forgiven. The horrific thought of breaking a piece of china that belonged to my mom was all of a sudden a little silly. A possession? Really? We are all that upset over a piece of clay? A little super glue and it would be back to normal. My sister felt horrible. My nephew balled his eyes out for being human, and my mom got over it. We laugh now at the possession comment, but I really think it was a deeper moment for all of us.

We all make mistakes. We all mess up big stuff, and we have a hard time finding enough super glue to put it all back together. Some things end up cracked and flawed, but we still love them anyway - even after trying to arrange all the pieces that have come our way. Sometimes, I think we arrange perhaps too much, instead of just letting things be. Sometimes, it's ok for there to be pieces as we navigate through life. Life is messy, and often it is simply too much for super glue to handle. The excuses are what keep those pieces from even being whole again.

And then we remember the guy who was burned almost to death and who lost the use of his limbs almost totally, no longer even having hands. Yet, he still plays the drums.

We remember the surfer with one arm after a shark attack who went on to win high level competitions.

We remember.

And then we make a choice.

We forget the possessions, and we focus on the heart and soul that truly measures us, or we make excuses about why we can't.

I think I am going to stop the excuses. I have laundry to do tomorrow. And I will thank God for giving me the legs and arms to carry it down the stairs.

I am living this day without excuses.

From now on, I am using the super glue only for the big stuff.

And arranging whatever pieces come my way, one at a time...

While I let the rest quietly slip away.

"Would you know how to feed yourself if you never knew the importance of food?"
He teased her with a question that seemed rhetorical. She wasn't sure how to answer.
"Just tell me what you are getting at? You speak in riddles. Just come out with it, I am tired of the games."
"Games? You think this is a game?"
He snickered, staring right into her steely-blue eyes.
She avoided his glare. She knew what happened when she really looked into them.
Deeply, with a sense of angst... she knew if she looked too long, she would see herself.
It was the one thing she feared the most.
"You know you won't get anywhere, right?" He was still staring at her.
She continued to stare at the centipede with the broken legs trying to climb up her boot. Futile, she thought.
Why wouldn't it stop trying? It obviously wasn't going to get up there.
"Right." She responded without taking her eyes off of the herculean effort she was witnessing.
She felt his glance move from her face to the dying bug on the ground next to her. It was still trying to climb.
She poked it with her finger, half in jest, half wondering if she did, could she help it move again?
Does this silly bug know it will die if it can't move to find food?
She chuckled to herself knowing the answer.
The angst set in again.

Chapter 32

Do you believe in miracles?

I spent the afternoon with my mom. She was good today, laughing at times and actually getting a couple words out. She looked at me across the table at one point and actually said "My baby." That meant the world to me. She really has no ability to say much of anything that we can understand. That gift today was a little miracle.

I sat and watched her as my aunt fed her lunch. Just being in the room made me feel an energy I cannot quite describe. I needed that. She reminded me of the importance of miracles. Her strength, her love, her ability to laugh in the face of her horrific disease is truly amazing and empowering to me. We sang Christmas carols and laughed. I walked out this afternoon loving my mom more than ever. She's my miracle.

I got back from Tennessee on Sunday night after spending Friday night in Chattanooga at the Fury Academy for a mental toughness seminar for players and coaches, and Saturday and Sunday in Knoxville for the University of Tennessee Christmas Softball Camp. After hours of talking about the mental game, I was in heaven. I can tell that I have a passion for the mental game, when I realized that after 14 and a half hours of speaking about the mental game over two days, I could have still talked about it even longer, if my voice had held up.

I spent Saturday and Sunday with 435 softball players, in 12 different sessions, with kids from ages 8 to18. I got through Saturday with the older groups. I had some great conversations and heard some really smart kids give some really good insights. Then Sunday came, and I started to think about how difficult talking to seven-year-olds about the mental game could potentially be - especially when I would be getting them at the end of a long two days. I braced myself for what could potentially be a rough day.

My sessions covered the make up of a champion. Five "C" words covered most of it. I spoke about Courage, Consistency, Composure, Character, and Confidence. I asked what each word meant to each of my groups. I heard some really great answers.

My favorite came in my 11th session, with the youngest girls all day, from one of the youngest girls in the group. She was the little girl in the front row, second seat. She was seven. Wearing her softball uniform proudly, her hand went right up when I asked what the word "Character" meant. I looked over to my right and saw her eyes looking back at me, almost as if she had an answer but also as if she wasn't totally sure about whether or not she was right. I called on her, walked over toward her and was not even close to being prepared for what I was about to hear. I said, "Yes... what do you think Character means?" She looked back, her eyes getting bigger... slowly putting her hand down, and with the sweetest, softest voice, she responded quietly yet deliberately.

"When you see a piece of trash... you pick it up?"

I was quiet for a minute, not really sure what just hit me. My heart felt so full. I smiled back, walked a little closer and immediately gave her a high five. I was amazed at her poise, and at her honesty and thought process. I said, loudly... "YES! That is perhaps the best answer I have ever gotten to that question." Thank you, seven-year-old little girl, for teaching ME that day.

I believe strongly that every day brings us small miracles. Miracles don't have to be a blind person seeing, or a disabled person suddenly being able to walk. Miracles sometimes come in small words, or even in moments that remind us of what our hearts feel and what they are capable of feeling. This time of year, we often talk about miracles, about believing in the magic of the season. I think it is so much more than just this one time of year. My mom's beautiful voice, trying to sing along to the songs we were singing, even without the ability of words. That little girl's courage to give an answer whether it was right or wrong... the beauty of these moments will live on in my heart always.

I watched a little boy on the airplane on my way home Sunday night bring joy to everyone close to him. He sat in the row next to me, on the other side of a businessman who was doing work on his laptop. The little boy was probably no more than four years old, with blond hair and big blue eyes. He was adorable. His mom was sitting next to him holding his younger brother.

We were about half way through the trip when the younger brother started to get fussy. His mom was getting a little flustered trying to tend to him, while also making sure that the older boy was ok. After a couple of minutes, the older boy turned to his mom and with the sweetest, most loving voice spoke. "Mom, it's ok. He's probably just tired." His mom looked at him and she could not resist smiling.. The businessman looked over at him and told him he was a pretty good big brother. Just then, we both watched as the older boy stroked his brother's head so gently and sweetly. He started to softly sing to him. "Twingle, Twingle, Widdle Staw." I saw the businessman crack a huge grin as the younger boy quieted down. Mom was smiling now. We were all smiling. It was a wonderful moment.

Miracles really can be just the smallest, most wonderful moments in life that we often don't have time to see or hear or even recognize. They are about being the right person... about recognizing love and allowing the small moments to be just enough.

So I ask of you now...

Do YOU believe in miracles?

Chapter 33

Reaching beyond what is required...

I was at Acme last night grabbing a few things to make my morning smoothies. Strawberries, blueberries, bananas, nonfat yogurt, you get the idea. Anyway, I was walking around looking for the little turkey sausages we have snacked on in the office, and I couldn't find them anywhere in the store.

Sometimes, I get weird cravings, and I had thought about them all day. I really had just started looking, but to be honest, I had NO idea where I might find them since the last time I got them they weren't in a place you would assume they would be.

There was an older gentleman rolling a large cart to stock the shelves down one of the aisles. I passed him, looking clueless I guess, because he asked me if I needed help finding something. I smiled and told him that I really wasn't sure where I would find what I was looking for, but perhaps he might know. I described the little turkey sausages I was craving as best I could, and he quickly set out on a mission to see if he could find me what I was looking for.

After about two minutes of quickly looking in some spots he thought might be the ones, he went and asked someone at the deli. They directed him to talk with Roberta, the lady who stocks that stuff. He went off to find Roberta. He came back maybe three minutes later, almost jogging back to me. He apologized about four times that they didn't stock them at that store. He told me that he asked Roberta, the lady who stocks them, and then he went and asked the scanner for the entire store to double check. After everyone confirmed that, no, they don't carry them, he came back and apologized that they didn't have them and that he was really sorry for making me wait.

I immediately looked at his nametag. "Charlie," it said. I glanced back to his eyes, big and blue, making his unkempt grey hair look like it was perfect. I smiled and thanked Charlie for everything he did to help me.

I walked away, but for some reason, I turned around again to watch him scurry back to the aisle he had left his stock cart in and get right back to work, busily making sure the cans of tomatoes perfectly lined up with each other, labels out and neat. I was struck by him. He was quick and efficient.

I smiled, nodded my head, and remembered that regardless of the job, setting himself apart was Charlie's way of doing things. He reached beyond what was required, no matter the task, and tried to do his very best. He wasn't able to find me my little turkey sausages, but it certainly wasn't because he didn't try.

About a week ago, my battery in my phone fried itself. I called Verizon Wireless to ask them to send me a new one. Some who know me may know of my trials and tribulations with my phones. I often feel like perhaps Candid Camera did an episode about me and I just haven't seen the reruns yet. I have spent a lot of time with Verizon technical support teams helping me with my issues.

I called to get my issue resolved this time and got a very pleasant voice. The person I spoke with was Michelle. She asked me what she could do to help me. I have heard that a thousand times before. I was hoping it would not be a huge dilemma to JUST get a new battery. She quickly made notes, put a request in for my battery and told me she would overnight it to guarantee delivery by 3:00 p.m. the next day so I would have it and not be without a working cell phone for too long. One and a half minutes, and I was off the phone. The battery was in my hand the next morning.

Michelle didn't do anything but her job that day, but her pleasant tone and quickness to please and take care of her customer made me feel like I was the most important thing in that moment. All of a sudden, I felt like perhaps all those sales meetings that taught us "customer service isn't a department it's an attitude," weren't so hokey after all.

What if we took that attitude beyond the job? What if that one percent extra would be what makes us stand out in our lives? What if that is what makes us be the one other people remember?

In sports, giving 100 percent is often the difference between the first and second place finisher. There is never any competition at the top... in business, in sports, really in life. Most people aren't in the top three percent in anything. Those are the ones who stand out. You know, the ones who do the extra lap in practice without being told, the ones who do the extra pushup when everyone else collapses, the one with the sheer determination to be just a little better than everyone else. Most of the world is content with being status quo. Mediocre. Mainstream. Maybe even complacent... don't rock the boat. You know the deal.

You may have heard of Pareto's Principle. The 80/20 rule, which states that 80 percent of the work is done by 20 percent of the people... "The difference between ordinary and extraordinary is just the little extra..." blah blah blah. I could go on and on with the clichés that describe this principle...and it's funny how there are so many. And maybe, just maybe, there is something in that too.

So, why did Charlie and Michelle stand out? Charlie didn't make something appear that didn't exist in his store, but he certainly would have if he could. Michelle didn't make something simple difficult when I was already frustrated at the battery dying when it was almost new. They just did their job - nothing more - but they did it gladly. They did it because their job was to help me in that moment.

My job is very much the same. Each moment, everyone has someone to "save," someone to run down a product for even if you come back empty-handed. Each someone has a moment, when in that moment that person is the most important thing in the world.

That kind of awareness of the world around me is who I strive to be every single day.

We are very much connected in that way.

Who knows, tomorrow you may be my Charlie.

I may be your Michelle.

Awareness is everything.

Awareness of reaching beyond what is required.

Chapter 34

Feel Fear... Do it Anyway

Have you ever been afraid? I mean, really afraid? Wondering if you really can do something you want to do? Afraid you may fail?

What is the root of fear? Some say FEAR is False Evidence Appearing Real. I say it's our mind doubting our own true potential. I think we all have greatness inside us. Every single person on this planet can make a difference. In fact... we all do... in one way or another; we affect each other in ways we will never see or know or comprehend.

So what is your greatest fear? I have read so much about the fear of failure. How it can handicap an athlete or a businessperson, or yourself... how it holds you back from what you so desire. Think about the one thing that you would do if you knew you couldn't fail. It takes courage to be a doer. It is easy to sit on the sidelines and watch. Perhaps one of my favorite quotes is the one on our office door at my previous company, ETC, Inc., by Theodore Roosevelt. It is so powerful, I am going to give you the whole thing:

"It is not the critic who counts; not the man who points out how the strong man stumbles, or where the doer of deeds could have done them better. The credit belongs to the man who is actually in the arena, whose face is marred by dust and sweat and blood, who strives valiantly; who errs and comes up short time and time again; because there is not effort without error and shortcomings; but who does actually strive to do the deed; who knows the great enthusiasm, the great devotion, who spends himself in a worthy cause, who at best knows in the end the triumph of high achievement and who at worst, if he fails, at least while daring greatly. So that his place shall never be with those cold and timid souls who know neither victory nor defeat."

What counts, what life is really about is showing up, every day, and doing the "thing" that has to be done... about daring greatly. It's about feeling fear, and doing it anyway. It's about looking fear in the face and pressing on—around, over and through, no matter how high or how deep.

Sometimes we fear that which we don't know... and even more often than not, we sometimes fear our greatest power being realized. It's called the fear of success. And you may be like me when I first heard that... you might be thinking "NO WAY!"... How can you be afraid to be successful? And I can tell you more so now than ever, I understand it. Pro athletes I have worked with have proven this to me. WE are more often afraid of being greater than we imagined than we are afraid of not being good enough. And sometimes, those fears work in tandem. They can handicap you. They often are what hold back even the greatest of success stories.

Awareness is number one. Know and understand what your fears are. So... what are you afraid of? Challenge yourself to do ONE thing you are afraid of today. You will realize in no time that it wasn't as scary as you first thought. Feel fear... Then do whatever you are afraid of anyway. And in the process, learn to love the newness of life. Because, after all, our greatness is what shapes us. And fear or not, we are made to realize it. Besides, what is the absolute worst thing that could happen?

Nothing, usually...

Chapter 35

Limits Begin Where Vision Ends...

Over the loudspeaker of the plane came the captain's voice: "We are about 20 minutes away from the airport; however, we just got word from air traffic control that the weather just got increasingly worse. Visibility is down to about 1/4 mile and we may have to divert to another surrounding airport." Sighs and groans filled the cabin, as a bumpy flight just got worse.

Typically, if you fly with me, stuff like that just happens. It seems like just a minor issue, the pilot not being able to see the runway, yes? Well, it certainly got me thinking... His next words were even funnier to me... "We are going to do all we can to land this thing here. Thankfully, they have long runways. Hope to talk to you when we are back on the ground."

I laughed... out loud actually, while the guy next to me was stressing out. I thought it was funny. And I reminded myself the pilot does this for a living. If he couldn't see, he wouldn't land us here, right? And then I started thinking about how often I have changed direction when I didn't see clearly, or when things just seemed too cloudy to "land."

Life can be funny that way. We start to see limitations where there once were none. We find reasons to doubt or to think that maybe what we thought existed really doesn't. Have you ever had a life changing moment? Where all of a sudden you realized that you were doing it all wrong? It's funny. I have had many of those moments, and I will continue to have them for as long as I am on this earth. As soon as we stop being able to see, things change. As soon as we lose sight of our reason, our strength, and sometimes even our weaknesses, we find that things aren't the same as they used to be. So we start to feel like we can't do it anymore, or we second guess even what we were doing in the first place. But we certainly don't want to burden others with our feelings.

There is tremendous happiness in making others happy, despite our own situations. Shared grief creates half the sorrow, but happiness, when shared, is so much more.

When we don't let the clouds overwhelm what we see that is right in front of us, we often find ways to see further. Don't take your "sight" for granted... whatever you may see is a blessing.

Our plane landed safely last Friday. Without much turbulence, as a matter of fact. And although it is great to be prepared, don't spend all your time worrying about what MAY happen.

You'll miss the view.

"Do you ever just stop? Take a break?" She had a slightly annoyed tone in her soft voice as she turned to address him.

He was always there.

He was always a frustrating presence to her especially when she really didn't want him to be there.

She couldn't escape the weight on her shoulders that he brought.

Always.

He was quiet.

She looked around once more and this time he didn't appear as usual.

"Here we go again," she whispered to herself.

"Come on... Come talk to me."

Her sing-songy voice was almost sarcastic.

Still. Nothing.

"I don't get it. You are never here when I need you. And then when I just want to be alone, you smother me like a blanket."

She sat, staring up at the clouds as they rushed past her, like the day was in fast-forward.

"Why do you doubt me?"

His voice startled her as it usually did. Out of nowhere and not when she expected it.

"Where have you been? I was talking to you before and you didn't hear me."

She was peering through the fog that had settled in, trying to find his eyes. She still couldn't see him.

"I heard you. You just doubted I was listening."

Chapter 36

I take nothing for granted.

Today, my eyes opened at 7:48 a.m. I looked at the clock, then closed them again and said "thank you."

Today was a normal day... like so many others, starting the same. With my eyes closed, I said a prayer for my mom, my family and my friends, that today will be a day of health and strength. It's my first thought. "Thank you." I live in abundance. Even the things that are missing in my life are not missing at all. They are there... they arrive just as I need them, and then go when I am finished with them. Even if I don't understand the timeframes... they come and go just the same. I say thank you for the negatives in my life, for the storms I have to learn to weather. I am not always sure how or why, but I know I am to learn from every experience I have and from everyone I have watched close to me as they lost people in their own lives.

Sometimes it is harder to watch someone else go through something difficult than it is to do so yourself. Often there are no words good enough to share your love and light in times of such darkness.

I sat beside my friend Laura and her family as they went through some of the darkest days they had known just four years ago when she lost her father. During that time, I remember walking into his hospital room while machines kept him alive until the organ donation could begin. I was alone. It was just him and me. I touched his hand and said goodbye. I shared my love for him and thanked him for being in my life.

During that visit, I was a witness to that moment in my life where I understood what it was to see pain, to hold it in my own hands, and to have no words to make it go away. I grew through the darkness and found light within the tragedy. I learned strength; I learned gratitude. I learned a deeper love for all that is unanswered along the journey.

I am thankful for Dad M. in my life. I am thankful for being a part of the process of his life and of his death. I don't take that highest level of learning for granted anymore.

I have countless times attended a funeral... saying goodbye to loved ones, wondering how my friends and family members who were directly affected on a daily basis could be so strong. I learn from all of them. I accept that loss is a part of life. I just struggle with the extreme pain some of us have to hold for as long as it takes.

A high school friend just recently lost her husband, the father of her child, to a car crash. Another lost his father, and another her favorite aunt all within a few weeks of each other. I sat by helpless as one of my players was killed in a car crash. She was too young to leave this earth. Her teammates were too young to have to grieve for someone their own age. That kind of pain is hard to justify. I feel badly that I have often felt so helpless.

Through the pain, we send love, and light, and hope, and prayers. It's what we do for each other. It's how we feel better about the fact that we can't change it, we can't bring them back. I don't take love and understanding for granted anymore.

There are times when I think about picking up the phone to say hi to someone I haven't spoken to in far too long. I get busy and often forget. Life goes by, and soon enough, it's years since we have talked. And then we realize that we have nothing to talk about anymore. So we just don't bother. And that becomes ok. And really, it is. As people and places come and go in our lives, we find ways to move on to something or someone else. Sometimes situations that once meant everything to us just don't serve us any longer. Most importantly, when we continue to be flexible and malleable in life, what we really find we can't take for granted is the safety and comfort we feel we need. Things change. People come and go, both by death and by choice. It's a part of the giant life cycle we are somewhere in the middle of. And instead of DOING, maybe if we just start BEING, we will embrace the changes as they happen. And then, only then, we won't take anything for granted anymore.

It's the prayer I will repeat again tomorrow morning. "Thank you."

Happy Thanksgiving... Every day.

Chapter 37

You can rewrite the story

Chapter One: The Dream.

I was seven when I wanted to be a teacher. It was cool for a moment. I felt I had something to give and I had a sincere sense of wanting to help others. Age eleven brought me the desire to be the next Barbara Walters. I wanted to be a reporter, to get the story and ask the hard questions. When I was 13 I dreamed of playing softball in the Olympics. I wanted to be the best at something. Age 17 saw me enter college as a Psychology major, wanting to help others once again, only to be told by my E110 teacher Colleen Webster that I was a writer. In the spring of 1992 I became an English major with a concentration in Journalism. Back to being Barbara Walters.

Then, a handful of "find myself" jobs brought me back to sports, coaching and ultimately to psychology. Receiving my Master's Degree in Sports Psychology, I came back to my previous decision about majoring in psychology. I spent time as an adjunct professor at Ursinus College... I guess that also brings me back to my very first desire of being a teacher. It's funny how life often completes the loop for us. There is something about closing the circle that makes me feel somewhat complete.

Chapter Two: The Reality.

Along that path of figuring out what I really wanted to be and do, I found the people who said I couldn't, or the ones who told me no. I heard I wasn't good enough. It was never my parents, or my teachers or my coaches who ever said any of that. It was in fact never anyone else telling me I wouldn't succeed. It was the story I was telling myself that held me back. It was me. And it was time I recognized it.

I opened a training facility. I won awards. I was recognized by others for successes and thanked for my ability to reach kids and make them feel special. I have always opened my camps and clinics with four rules. We hustle all the time, we respect each other, we keep things fun always, and we NEVER use the word "can't." Perhaps that fourth one came from my strong desire to correct my own weakness and my own inability to stop saying it to myself. I have invited those I teach to use "I just haven't mastered it yet" instead. Because some day, we all have the ability to rewrite the story. But it has to start with the words we dream up in our own heads.

Coaching athletes, I often resort to these reminders. When we say "I can't." We believe it. We limit our potential. We make life hard because we say it is.

We don't need to. That's the funny part. We don't need to make things anything but simple. Because, when you take the pieces apart, we find they really are not as complex as we conjured them up to be. One idea, one thought, one "I can" moment all of a sudden changes things. Our minds turn a corner.

I often ask athletes to breathe this in, to let go of negatives and hold on to the dreams we had when we entered into the role of being an athlete. To rewrite the story we tell ourselves is simple. It just takes a little faith, a little less of what we think is reality, and a lot more of the dreams we had as that seven-year-old little kid.

Chapter Three: The Dream.

I am a teacher. I am a coach. I am a writer. I am a speaker. And every day I wake up, I decide my mood. I choose the feelings I get to have as I get out of bed. I am creating my own story. Based on all the things I have wanted to be, all the things I decided I could be, I have changed the can'ts to cans and have allowed my dream to take it's own shape and direction. Whatever I have yet to accomplish in my life is completely up to me. I have more choices than I often thought I did.

When we grow older, we don't actually always grow wiser. I would take my mind as a seven year old any day. My ability to dream and act as if. The ability to see the things I want to do and not see any of the self-constructed barriers.

Perhaps it's because I am facing a birthday at the end of this week that I am reflecting on my own story. Like when I was seven or eleven or thirteen, I have a dream of what I will be someday. And I have once again invited the dream and reality to be one in the same.

No one told me I couldn't.

Chapter 38

Taking the road less traveled.

Today, I became a better person; just because I decided. I spent my morning at a Community Leaders lunch with the Chester County Communities That Care program. I listened to amazing people share their stories and their reasons why they are involved in this awesome program that gives back to our community's youth in ways I never even knew. It's not always easy to stand up in front of a group of people and admit your weaknesses. But I had an opportunity today to listen to Christopher Kennedy Lawford (an actor, author, activist, and leader) speak about his trials and tribulations growing up as a drug and alcohol addict and it moved me. I took the time to speak to him one on one afterward, to thank him for taking time out to come to Downingtown, PA, today and for his path to cross mine. I know meeting him was supposed to happen today. Today, I became a better person.

You see, most people take the easy way out; me included. So often, it is easier to just do what everyone else is doing, to say nothing, to sit idly by and cheer from the stands. It's easier to not admit you are human. It's easier to not show your vulnerability. It's easier to sit, stagnant, and wait for something to come along to make you HAVE TO change direction. It's easier to just be. And whatever happens, will happen. I, too, have heard myself say that often.

And we leave things up to chance. We think fate hands us whatever we get. And while sometimes we aren't in control of what happens to us, we are ALWAYS in control of how we react to it.

Sometimes, we take the road with all the traffic, where everyone else is stuck, too. And we curse the fact that we aren't moving anywhere, that there are too many cars on this road. And it was OUR choice. Other times, we would just rather be on the dirt path that no one else knows exists, just so that we can keep moving. We take the road less traveled. We explore; we find new ways. We blaze a trail. We become better people.

I watched my (and yes, when I invest myself into a team, they become mine, too) UHS LAX girls play a tough game last night. I watched the emotion after the game. I watched them all make choices. We talked today about how this is a pivotal and critical choice, a defining moment as an athlete. This is when they decide whether to pick themselves up and fight again or lay there defeated. Still. No movement… the easy way out. Stuck in traffic with everyone else. Or we can take the road less traveled. I know what they are going to do. I am excited to see them blaze a trail. They have all the tools they need to become better players.

When I was in college at the University of Delaware, my "senior seminar" class was with one of my all-time favorite professors. You had to apply to get in the class, and you had to write a thesis at the end of the semester and present or teach a class by yourself in order to graduate.

As an English major with a concentration in journalism, I LOVED creative writing. Poetry was my favorite. When I saw my favorite professor was the moderator for the class, I quickly applied. I submitted some of my work and the essays needed to show you could understand the writings of some of the greatest poets of all time. We spent a lot of time in that class talking about some of my favorites. My thesis was a comparison and contrast between a Dylan Thomas work and an Emily Dickinson piece. My professor told me that no one had compared the two I had chosen before. I liked that. No one had gone before me. I got to blaze the trail. And while it was hard, and there was no one to help me, I got to set the standard. There was no one who could have been better than me until then. It was kind of a great spot to be in, if you ask me.

We spent a few weeks of class talking about the great American poet Robert Frost and all of his more obscure poems. Then, we got to this one: "The Road Not Taken." I don't think there are many people - in my world at least - who have not heard it. The funny thing is, since all 11 of us in the class had read it a thousand times and we certainly had seen it in prior English and poetry classes, we figured it would be a quick discussion and we would move on.

We were wrong.

There was nothing quick about Professor Gibbons Ruark. He was a man of his own tempo. He walked into each poetry class and stood in front of the room until it got quiet. He would then recite a random poem - so beautifully every time. I lived for the beginning of his classes, to hear his deeply passionate voice, to see his scruffy and sometimes unkempt self. He WAS poetry. He didn't care what people thought or who may have snickered when he walked by. He was Doctor Ruark, and anyone who knew him, loved him.

Our discussion lasted for two different two-and-a-half- hour classes. On that one poem - the one we all thought we knew and understood. He made us see other things than we ever realized were there. He gave us a choice to see what everyone else saw or to take another look at it - A deeper look – and see what others did not see: A road less traveled.

I think what Dr. Ruark and even Robert Frost wanted us to learn was that no matter whether good or bad, EVERY choice you make will make a difference in your life. You most likely will miss out if you choose one alternative over the other, but "as way leads onto way," we move on, and we cannot focus on the things we didn't do… the paths we didn't go down. Dr. Ruark showed us in that class of his that sometimes, things aren't always what you think.

And so it is. We choose how we react to everything. We choose our path. We choose what we can control. And the rest we let go.

We can't worry about the paths we don't take. We can focus only on the ones we do. We can be true to who we are and we can honor our own humanity by acknowledging our mistakes and imperfections. There is beauty in that. And in that beauty, we become better people.

There is strength in taking the road less traveled.

Join me.

Chapter 39

Today, my hero is you…

I spent an hour and a half yesterday with a high school girls' lacrosse team that certainly knows how to win. I sat in the room and listened as they spoke openly, rallied around each other, and shared emotion that moved me. They didn't know it, but it moved me. I walked out when we were done feeling refreshed. YES, this is what being a part of a team is about, I thought, almost out loud. There were many heroes in that room yesterday - The quiet ones, the outspoken ones, the ones who laughed and those who cried. The words; the silence. The thoughts, the understanding… they were all heroes.

I believe that every team has a hero. But it's often not just one person… it's many. And…sometimes a hero isn't even a person at all. It's a feeling. It's a moment. It's when a bond can't be broken. It's an unspoken look, it's an electricity that sometimes has no words. It's trusting that no matter what, you can't fail because it's not just about you anymore. A hero is not an isolated incident; it's not scoring the winning goal or hitting the winning homerun. It's the quiet moments, the ones that may not count in the scorebook. It's being the person to step aside sometimes and letting someone else get the spotlight.

There is a lacrosse team out there playing hero... I am glad to have been in the room with them. Today, my hero is you. And you had no idea...

I drove back to my facility after my meeting with the lacrosse team, and on my way I was listening to my iPod. Unmistakably, as my life has its own way of giving me signs that sometimes even I couldn't miss, no matter what, the song "Hero" by Mariah Carey came on. I have loved that song since it first came out, and I often refer to it as one of my all time favorites. I know, I am dating myself... but it's a song that had a lot of meaning in my earlier life and, to this day, it creates feelings of being the right person for others. Sometimes, we are the hero. Sometimes, we surround ourselves with them so we can let another light shine.

On my way up the road, I was slowed by a lot of traffic. Having a moment of "Ugh, not traffic again" because I was stuck in other traffic on my way to my meeting with the lacrosse team earlier, I had a flash of annoyance come over me.

Then, all of a sudden, it hit me. I realized the reason for the traffic was. I had read earlier that there would be a lot of traffic in the area due to an historical event going on here right here in my little down of Coatesville.

Just then, police directed me to me to turn down a side road to take a detour. I was on a hill and I could oversee the entrance to Lukens Steel. I quickly pulled over and got out of my car, almost as if I was having an out of body experience. I was standing on the side of the road with a handful of other onlookers before I knew it, and I watched as the last of a 28-truck convoy drove slowly into the entrance. They were carrying a load of steel girders on each truck - 500 tons in all. But this wasn't just any steel... most days, trucks carrying steel would not stop traffic and bring people out to watch. This steel just happened to be the frame that was built 40 years ago at this very same plant where it was coming home. And the frame was from the first nine floors of the World Trade Center buildings.

As I stood and watched, American flags draping the trucks, ladder trucks spanning the road with a flag the convoy rode under, I couldn't help but think of the hundreds of lives lost on that one gut-wrenching day on September 11, 2001. As I have written about before, the close ties to both my family and my friends affected by that tragedy will be forever ingrained in my mind and on my heart. I know we will never be the same. I certainly will never be the same. But it is because of the many heroes who gave of themselves, that so many people survived.

I was lucky not to lose my sister that day. And as I watched that last truck drive under the American flag, I had tears in my eyes knowing that those pieces of steel represented a whole list of other people who played hero that day. And I thanked them.

Today, my hero is you. And you have never even met me.

I was in the Turkey Hill tonight picking up some milk on my way home. There was a man with his son standing by the ice cream case. When I turned the corner, I saw a little girl standing next to the boy holding his hand. She was probably about four, and he was probably no more than seven or eight. While his dad was picking out his flavor, the boy looked down at his sister and asked her what kind of ice cream she wanted. She pointed. The boy reached in and got it out of the freezer, holding onto her hand the whole time. Just then, the doll she was holding by the hair fell out of her hand and into the freezer. She started to cry at the thought of her doll freezing to death, so the boy quickly reached down in and grabbed it before it could get as much as a slight chill. He quickly turned to her, and in that moment, the most beautiful expression I have ever seen on a little boy's face caught my eye.

"Miss Lizzy is ok, Jess. I saved her." And right then, the flavor of ice cream didn't much matter. Jess had a hero holding her hand.

Today, my hero is you.

A seven-year-old little boy who didn't even know I was there.

So, what about those lacrosse girls? They won tonight. I sat in the bleachers watching a team that knows HOW to be a team. And after the game, I made my way across the field to give some high fives to them. Instead, I got a huge group hug from them. In that moment, I remembered, again, why I do what I do. Or more importantly, why I LOVE to do what I do. The excitement, the chemistry, the feeling of a team: it's all MY hero.

Only a few seconds passed as I was walking toward them, and they were running to hug me... ALL OF THEM... Little did they know the impact of that simple gesture. They thanked me for coming to cheer them on and for the time we spent together only yesterday.

But little did they know...

Heroes aren't built on other's shoulders, they are not always seen or recognized. They can be fleeting moments we walk right by.

Seconds of awe and inspiration if we so choose to acknowledge and our reflection is far-reaching.

The hand we hold, the smile we cast, the candle we light when all others' have gone out.

Today... My hero is you.

Chapter 40

Fall Down; Get Up Again.

Have you ever watched a child learn to walk? Their first few steps… holding on to anything in sight…the coffee table, chair, mom's pant leg, dad's knee… legs wobbling underneath their unsteady bodies? The first step away from the steadiness of holding on…the first step alone?

Yeah, you know what happens next… The fall, the sounds of diaper hitting the floor, padding the landing… Hand out, grabbing, searching for something to pull themselves back up. And back on unsteady legs within four seconds flat to try again. How many times have you seen this? And how many times have you thought about the fact that these children quite simply don't know any better. They just get up and try again. And again. And again. It's called fearlessness. It's what we all had at some point. It was our first huge hurdle in our lives, learning to walk. We fell down, and we didn't question doing it over and over.

So where did we all of a sudden forget how to get back up again? Things happen in our lives, and we feel defeated. We fall down, and we stay down. Not only do we stay down, but we bring a pillow and blanket and just sleep on the floor. We make it as comfortable as we possibly can down there, since we will be staying for a bit. And only when we are good and ready, and the floor is no longer comfortable, or it's too cold, do we decide to try to get up again. And if we aren't successful, oh well. It doesn't matter any more, because we left the pillow and blanket there to keep us comfortable just in case.

We fall; we get up. And the true measure of success is not in how many times you fall, but in how many times you get back up. If you make it a point to get up one more time than you fall down, you can be that child again. It's no different. We think it's such an amazing feat... that it takes such strength and courage. No, sometimes it actually just takes mindless activity.

Fall down. Get up again. It's that simple.

Part Five.

Faith

"There comes a time when we look around and see nothing, know nothing, and have no sense of belonging. It is then that we find solace in the questions and even the empty answers. It is the gift of a knowing in our gut that transcends all else. They call it faith. I call it home."
-- jlc

The skyline was blurry when she tried to find him. She couldn't see his outline; nor could she hear his steps behind her as she usually did. She stopped in the clearing to navigate.

"Hello?" she whispered as she heard a twig snap a few feet behind her.

"Are you there?"

No response.

Again, a twig and some crumpling of leaves... then, another twig.

"I don't see you."

"You won't." His voice was almost transparent... on the wind like a strong whisper that sent chills down to her cold, bare feet.

"Where are you? I can't..."

"Shhhhhh." He paused.

She stopped talking.

"You won't see me. You can only feel me."

"Why? You were here before... I touched your hand. You gave me things. Why can't I see you now." Her voice grew increasingly impatient, speeding up as if she was running out of breath to push the words out.

"I don't understand... Why are you doing this to me?" She shook from the chill in the air as the sun had descended 49 minutes before. She shook from the fear of navigating these dark woods alone. She shook because she knew what was coming next. She knew.

"You just have to trust. I am here. I always have been. I always will be. You can't live without me. "

The truth was stark and somewhat hard to hear. If she was going to get through these next few paths, she needed to trust that life wouldn't lead her astray.

"Ok," she managed to squeak out through the fear in her mouth.

"I trust you. Even if I can't see you."

She turned around and walked into the clearing. The sun was bright.

Darkness was behind her. Life appeared from the rays and took her hand. The grip loosened, the path was clear, the sound of his voice rang in her mind like never before.

"Welcome home, Jen."

Chapter 41

Faith is in the knowing...

She looked out from behind the Local News section of the Bergen Record.

"It will work out... don't worry."

"But what if..."

"STOP," she begged in her calm voice.

"You don't have to worry about it. It will all be taken care of. Sometimes you just need to have a little faith."

She turned to find page B4, where the story continued.

I slowly walked away, wanting so badly to ask again... to find out if maybe she would know or could find out when... If maybe she had known something I did not, causing my doubt and worry to creep in.

I did not want to miss out on a thing... I wanted to know. When my shoes would arrive? When dad would be home with the car? When we were leaving to go to dinner so I could make plans around it? How I was getting to practice? What did I need to do next weekend?

I carried that worry and the constant need to know what and how into my adult life. Together, they became an anchor I would soon identify as my very own. It was a part of my perfectionism. I needed it just as Linus needed his blanket, or more like someone needs a long fall from a short pier. I needed to realize quickly that I didn't really need it at all. The letting go was like pulling a bottle away from an infant who hasn't eaten in five days. I clung to it as if I wouldn't breath if I somehow rid myself of the very thing that had fed me.

Letting go is sometimes the hardest thing we ever do in life. Even if it's letting go of the very thing that is building the wall in front of us.

I found that wall pop up again as recently as a few months ago. In a very dark and deeply saddened few weeks, I allowed myself to watch as despair, failure, desolation, worthlessness, and fear laid each brick, piling higher and higher right in front of me. I watched and didn't say a word. I let it build, almost as if I was cheering on those very bricks that would soon be my cell walls. I certainly didn't stop it.

And then I was reminded in one moment by one voice that I was stronger than that wall. I was reminded that I didn't need to let the cell close me in. There were only three walls... I could certainly retreat and go back out the way I came in. BUT... I tried to argue with failure by reminding him that I came from that way and that if I go back I MUST be doing it all wrong. I tried to reason with despair, telling her that if I could get it right just one time, I may feel ok about myself.

Stress, worry, failed relationships and hurting friends and a difficult family situation is enough to set me on a path to become a professional bricklayer.

But that's too easy. That's where my belief could have led me. I could go down a path and build walls around myself. I wondered what and how and when… and been happy on those so called "stress-less days" and spent the rest of my time chasing my worries around the cul-de-sac of the next dead end road.

But belief won't write my story, at least not the way I want it to read.

Faith is stepping out into the darkness and knowing, without question, that things will fall into place when you need them to the most, that the bricks will not know how to fasten to each other. The world ran out of mortar. And when the time comes to go over, around or through those walls, there is no question. We choose the roads without worry. We walk our path without fear. Despair fell after the last strong wind, and failure never even made it to the road the wall was on.

We choose our path. We know life will give us one hell of a ride. We have faith the ride doesn't have to include a crash ending.

Faith is in the knowing.

And I don't really have to explain it anymore…

Chapter 42

What I am is enough...

Her questioning blue eyes reflected the sunrays coming in through the ripped shade in the kitchen. The hole in it was just enough to make her squint.

"Why are some people policemen while others are drug dealers? And why are some lawyers while others are prostitutes? Do the people who settle for less than they are know they could be more?"

He looked down into those blue eyes that spoke out loud. Without saying a word, he just held her gaze for what seemed like an hour. It was only 3 seconds.

"Yes baby… I don't know. But that's a real good question. How did you get so smart so young?"

She was annoyed by his patronizing of her childish question. He was embarrassed that he didn't know how to answer his 9-year-old daughter.

"I wish I knew," He managed to choke out.

She knew.

She knew all along.

And all those years later, when she remembered the conversation vividly, she knew that was the turning point in her life. A nine-year old who knew what she wanted to be, and more importantly a nine-year old who knew she could be more than she would eventually settle for.

A failed relationship. A suicide thought. Countless losses of those close. The death of a loved one, so quickly and so young. A miserable living. Hating work, hating home, hating everything that she touched. Maybe she didn't know anymore.

That nine-year old convinced her otherwise.

A failed marriage. A sick parent. A dying friend. And then, it was clear.

She stopped listening to her. The nine-year old was screaming on mute. The closed caption, turned off. The ability to understand or read lips or even want to know was slipping away.

She lost everything. Or so it seemed.

When all of a sudden, her mirror opened, much like her heart again for the 17th time. The "Maybe it will work out this time" mantras started to beat their tattered drum.

And all of a sudden she turned and faced the mirror on a nondescript Wednesday and caught those nine-year old eyes in the mirror. "Do the people who settle for less than they are know they can be more?"

And the truth shot back like a piercing reflection.

She knew.

She knew all along.

Chapter 43

Go with your heart...Always.

Choices. Integrity. Words. Truth. Communicating what's real. Doing what's right. It's not always easy to stand up to those who are on other sides of the issues. It's not always fair to be the one to have to tell the truth. And sometimes, even when it's a no-brainer... you will look around at all those who said they had your back, and when everyone else is walking away, you stand alone.

These are every day occurrences, whether we notice them or not. Choices begin with getting out of bed and move on to what we wear, to if we should eat breakfast, and eventually end with what time we go to bed and whether we should sleep on our back or our stomach or our side... We make these choices every day. Some are completely inconsequential; others... life-changing. We choose to stand up for what we believe in... or we crumble under the pressure of those who don't stand at all. We choose to be real and speak true, and be strong in the face of weakness. It is our choice that matters. It is our heart that leads us.

I was faced with a moment in middle school that seemed quite insignificant at the time, but later in life it proved to be just the beginning of my sometimes too outspoken self. There was a new girl that yea; it was 7th grade… and we will call her "Clara."

Clara transferred in from another school, and she didn't know anyone. Kids being usual bullying kids picked on her because she was new. I am sure she was not happy with the choice her parents made for her that first day in a new school. At one point, in fifth period, I remember she left the room crying. I immediately stood up and asked the teacher if I could go make sure she was ok. I don't know why, but my heart felt like it was the right thing to do. I walked out of the room before I even got an answer. She was sitting alone, in the stairwell sobbing. I sat next to her and put my arm around her shoulder. I didn't say a word. I just wanted to let her know that someone was there. I made a choice. I went back in the classroom and told the two boys who were picking on her to knock it off. That was probably the first time I ever stood up to someone like that in front of others.

And even if I stood alone, I would do it the same every time. I learned a long time ago what integrity was. One of my favorite quotes is by Oprah Winfrey: "Real integrity is doing the right thing, knowing that nobody's going to know whether you did it or not." Integrity is who you are behind closed doors, when you don't get the credit and the spotlight isn't on. Integrity is what you say when no one is there to hear it and back you up. Integrity is doing the right thing… no matter what. Integrity is believing in your heart what is right… and following through with action. Integrity needs no introduction, or explanation. It just is. And when you let your heart lead, you get to the center of what that is.

I know some people think that if you don't do what your mind tells you to do, you are not acting rationally. I say that's an excuse for not wanting to get hurt. I ask those same people to think of some of the greatest leaders throughout history… Gandhi, Martin Luther King, Jr., Rosa Parks, Princess Diana, Mother Teresa, Bono… I am sure there are not many people you can find who don't know these names. And why…? Why do we list the same kinds of people every time we talk about great leaders and great people…? They have integrity. They have led with their heart. And people followed.

Every day, we make choices. Some are completely inconsequential. Others… life-changing.

Regardless of impact or outcome, do what real leaders do …

Go with your heart … always.

Chapter 44

In the darkest hour... light.

"Who is more foolish, the child afraid of the dark or the man afraid of the light?" ~Maurice Freehill

There were moments, growing up in a big old house, that I admit I didn't want to go up to bed alone. I don't really know why... but the dark had its way of gripping me tightly and making my heart beat a little faster than normal. So I wonder... what was it I was afraid of? There were no monsters or creatures that hid under my bed or in my closet. I was sure to check out the probable hiding spaces quite often. The unknown factor was so broad, and so vague... it always is, isn't it? We are afraid of what we cannot see... what we don't know to be fact. What "might" be hiding beyond the light.

There are days I feel that now. And nights that just seem darker than usual. The moon sometimes takes away just enough of the darkness, but it keeps me wondering what is out there, beyond what I can see at night.

I know as you read this, if I ask you to think about one of your darkest moments, you can find it pretty easily. We all have those. We all find different sources of light to take us out of those moments or days, or even months and years. And at the risk of sounding trite, without one we would never know or even understand the other.

I often try to look at life as a cycle, as a day fades to night, and then back to day… or fall turns cold and dark and winter then becomes spring again. We can't stop it from happening, no matter how hard we try… with or without us in the world, the sun will come up again tomorrow morning, and these last few weeks of winter will soon fade to green leaves and buds on the trees. No matter what we do… it will happen.

As it is with our own "mini-seasons" or days, our own lives that we experience good, bad or indifferent. The darkest days always find glimmers of sunlight. And in time, we find that perhaps what we thought was dark, really wasn't, and that even when the sun goes down, the moon is bright. Sometimes, in the darkest hour, if we just look beyond our own shadow, we realize there is light in everything. There is a chance to be uncomfortable in the process, and in that… having faith that the light will come. In some way, and in some form… The darkness won't last.

I still may not want to go to bed alone tonight. I may check the closet and under the bed, just to make sure. And when I turn out the light, I may keep my eyes open just long enough to see the moon falling through my window, reminding me that the sun will be there when I open my eyes again. What I may not be able to see and what I don't know do not matter now.

Because even tonight, even in the darkest hour… comes the light.

"What are you thinking about? I can see you are trying desperately to fall asleep."

He knew she was restless and seemed a bit uncomfortable.

She lay there, wondering what to say.

She could be honest and let him know all of her worries and fears.

Or, she could say it's nothing, like she usually does, and just try to go to sleep.

She didn't move. Hoping he wouldn't ask again, she could just pretend she was already sleeping.

He knew better. He always does.

"Do you want to talk about it?"

She rolled over and tried one more time to get comfortable.

To no avail.

"If I knew, wouldn't I be laying here, tossing and turning."

He watched her discomfort grow.

She turned again.

"Maybe you just need a pillow. A comfortable one. That one is almost non-existent."

She laughed, thinking of the stack of pillows she has in the closet. The ones she tried and after a week needed a new one.

The ones that failed the comfort test.

And the ones that were just flat out awful.

She stacked them up thinking one day she may be able to reuse them.

He sat on the hard wood floor under the window and fell asleep.

Immediately.

Chapter 45

You always come full circle...

TO COME FULL CIRCLE (Dictionary.com): To make a complete change or reform; To complete a cycle of transition, returning to the point of origin.

And so it was... back to New Jersey for me a few weekends ago to visit friends and family... back to my roots, where I started my softball career, where my life changed; where I became who I am today.

I drove over to my high school, and as I pulled into the parking lot behind the school, I remembered immediately what it felt like to be there. I walked over the little bridge to see something completely different than what I remembered. It all changed. Everything changed. The school was added onto... the fields were moved and repositioned. It was nothing like when I was there 20 years ago. But I still found myself walking through the grass with the feelings I got on game day. Taking a deep breath to take it all in, I found solace in the fact that after all these years, I still feel the same way when my feet touch a softball field - passion... unbreakable, real, true passion for the game.

So while I have certainly made a complete change, and I am

sure in a few different ways... in my lifetime since those days at that little high school in my small suburban town just outside of New York City, I have also found so many times where my life has come full circle, completing that cycle of transition and returning to the point of origin... my life... in a nutshell.

I am older, wiser (at least I like to think I am), more open to learning; softer, tougher, truer to myself... But I will never, ever forget where I came from.

It's not a crazy story by any means... nothing like those who have spent their time in inner city ghettos finding their way out and into something more. Or like that of someone who was orphaned and grew up with next to nothing. Or someone who had a long line of abuse or drug use or some other horrible negative they had to overcome. NO... it wasn't like that. I was an average kid who played sports, grew up in a good family with a roof over my head. Nothing spectacular. I am here, full circle.

And so it goes. Life happens; it moves on, and you find new things to fulfill you. You move forward to move backward... and backward to move forward. And the merry-go-round keeps turning. Some days it spins faster than others... some days you just long to get off and others have a deep want and desire to get back on... and around and around it goes.

So as I see my life in places return to the point of origin, I will never forget where I came from. I won't ever forget the feeling I get when I take myself back to a spring day in 1990, toeing the rubber, knowing the game was on my shoulders. I look back now, and I find such strength in the little moments of victory. I have taken them with me from that field at Tenafly High School in that little town in New Jersey. I have learned from every moment I have lived so far.

No beginning and no end...

You always come full circle.

Chapter 46

It is not THIS day...

A day may come when my desire and need to help others disappears... but it is not THIS day. Today, I choose to be aware of those around me, regardless of my own place in the world. Some days, we are tired. Some days, we are sick. Some days, we don't even really feel like getting out of bed. But regardless of where I find myself today, I choose to want to give. It is my human obligation.

Watching the news today was a not-so-gentle reminder of how quickly life can change, how fragile this earth and all of us on it in fact are. We do not choose natural disaster... but we can choose how we feel, how we respond and how we live the lives we have been blessed with. Not just any day... but TODAY. Today we choose that. We are all here, living and breathing and sharing. I choose this day to share with you.

A day may come when my integrity doesn't lead my life...but it is not THIS day. Today, I choose to act in a way that creates strength. It is a way of being, not ever questioning if it feels right in my gut. Integrity is who I am when I am sitting alone in my office, behind a closed door, with a strong desire to make someone else's life just a little bit easier. It is thinking and doing that coincide. It is following through with what I have said I would do. It is commitment. It is being true to my vision and true to the mission statement on my wall that I stare at every day. It is challenging myself to go further, push harder, and make more of an impact as long as it benefits others.

A day may come when passion is no longer important...but it is not THIS day. Today, I choose passion to drive me. I find the burning desire in my gut to create, to think, to give of myself. When asked what my favorite word is, I always answer "Passion." It's the center of all things that have any meaning to me. I truly believe that some people float through life more at the surface of the world, who experience only some of what that feels and looks life, while others spend time in a deeper place, living and loving more passionately, more deeply... with a greater negative impact though when things hurt. However, I would gladly allow myself to hurt more if I could experience a deeper and more intense passion.

A day may come when I choose mediocrity over excellence... but it is not THIS day. Today, I choose to honor those around me and those who have gone before me by giving my best to every piece of my day. I choose to smile more at others, to listen more intently, to understand without having to be understood. Today, THIS day, I choose to make an impact for someone else- by a phone call, a gesture of encouragement to someone who is struggling, or by a re-commitment to striving for more than just being ok. Some days get busy. We fly through life like a machine, getting things done, going to bed and doing it all over again the next day.

Today, I remind myself to slow down, to think about how my hectic life impacts those around me.

A day may come when my courage fails...but it is not THIS day.

It is so easy to allow fear to take control, to let it climb in the driver's seat and keep me from taking another step into the unknown. It is so easy to allow feat to destroy my faith, to make me question who and why and how and when. It is so easy to allow it to steer me off track and down a road that I didn't want to be on. Fear reminds me that sometimes I need to be ok with just not knowing… with allowing life to unfold in it's own time and to take the wheel when I am ready. Fear begets courage. Always.

And I know that if that day ever comes, we already had this conversation.

I will be waiting…

I will be prepared…

And I will not worry about it until it happens.

Because I am sure…

It is not THIS day.

Chapter 47

Do You Believe in Santa?

It was Christmas, 1978. I was five. And sick... I couldn't go out on our yearly drive around the neighborhoods to see the lights so we weren't there when Santa came to deliver gifts.

You see, growing up, we opened presents on Christmas Eve at night, after church... We stayed up 'til the wee hours of the morning, then slept in while we waited for Dad to come home from doing the Christmas morning church service. Then we had Christmas breakfast together and then it was time to play with the cool toys we got the night before.

But that year, 1978, I was sick... So my mom or my sister – I can't remember which - ushered me up to my bed to try to get me to sleep before Santa got there. For some odd reason, Santa must have been shy or something, because we were never allowed to see him... or her... or whomever Santa "really" was, or "he" wouldn't leave the presents. So I laid in my bed, excited and thinking that maybe THIS was the year I would get close enough to hear him come in the house.

We didn't have a chimney, so apparently we left the door unlocked for Santa to make his way in... not safe, I know, ...

but we couldn't risk missing him and him not being able to get in...

All of a sudden, I heard bells... and a loud "HO, HO, HO,"... which still, to this day, reminded me a little of my sister Judy. But nonetheless, I was wide-eyed with amazement that I could hear Santa in my living room. A few rustles of bags, and he was gone. I snuck out of my room to see if my cookies were edible, and sure enough, they were... there were just a few crumbs left. Santa had been here – while I was trying to sleep upstairs

All these years later, I still remember my brush with Mr. Claus, and I know how lucky I was to have the gift of hearing him in my house, bells and all. I have always believed in Santa. And I probably do even more so today than ever.

I saw him in the eyes of a soldier when I was riding the shuttle bus at the airport. He got up for a woman who didn't have a place to sit, not looking for a thank you, which was good because the woman didn't even look his way... She just sat down and continued to talk on her phone. I smiled at him and thought... yes... that is what Christmas is about. Doing things for others and not looking for anything in return. Santa was in camouflage that day.

I saw him last week in a store in the eyes of a young child who was so excited to show her mommy a toy. "Look at this mommy!!!!" It was like Christmas happened right there at that moment, on that day... just for her. It was all she ever wanted. Her mommy responded with a "Why don't we wait and see if Santa brings it for you..." Her smile didn't fade one bit... it just meant that she had to wait a few days and the magic of Santa would give her enough hope that she might just get what she wanted. She was almost more excited about that proposition than the toy itself. Santa was there with them both in that store. I just KNOW .

I heard him in the voice of my little nephew Tommy wishing everyone a "Merry Christmas" on a voicemail. The tone and the words were just perfect, and they helped me to know that Santa was there with him, too.

I felt him in my family's hugs on Friday. All of us were together in one place… probably the first time in a LONG time that this has happened. It just felt good and right and it felt like love. Santa definitely made his way through each of us.

I heard him in the "thank you's" from the Coatesville Food Co-op when I delivered a truck load of food two weeks ago. As I walked inside, the tables had three packages of food left to give out, and a whole long list of families to give them to. My truckload filled two big shopping carts with food, enough to feed the list for the next two weeks they said. Santa was there that day, too.

I feel him when I sit here at this desk, thinking about the lives we have to touch… the smiles we have to give… the lessons we have to learn AND teach. I am blessed by those around me, those who work here with me and those who come through the doors for us to teach. I learn from each and every one of them, and I am honored to be amongst a whole long list of Santa's. They are here, day in and day out.

I believe in Santa, every day, all year round. He is present in all we do, in the magic, the belief, the faith. Santa is the gift of today and the hope of tomorrow and the not knowing what kind of magic awaits us around the corner. Yes, I do believe in Santa.

He is present. I have heard him. I have seen him. I know him well.

"I've done all I can do."

The thought became a sword that she would slowly pull out of her chest.

"I have nothing left."

The sword was dripping, the hole deep.

She sat, wallowing the minutes away.

Until that moment.

There he was, standing before her in all his armor.

She couldn't touch him if she tried.

"What are you afraid of?"

Even completely protected, he whispered like a scared seven-year-old child in the dark.

"Afraid?" She shook her head as she managed to push the word out of her lips.

He crept closer.

She grasped around for the sword that just a minute ago was imprinted in her heart.

Her empty hand matched the way her heart had been feeling the last three and a half minutes.

"How did you know?"

He moved closer.

Her hand and heart without a weapon.

She grasped in the darkness again without reaching anything.

Something.

Nothing.

She just wanted to feel whole again.

She wanted him to remove the sword.

"That's not my job," he replied, even softer than before.

He knew what she was thinking.

She couldn't understand how.

He reached out to her with his hands open, his armor a loud reminder of her inability to strike back.

"There's more. You always have more. Get up now and continue on. There's always more."

The clanking of the sword fell to the cement floor.

It startled her as she opened her eyes to the sun peeking through the curtains.

The sound echoed all morning.

Chapter 48

Open your eyes and see...

There is a difference between seeing and having vision. There is a difference between looking and seeing. Sometimes there are things that are right in front of you that you forget to "see"... we all do it, looking and looking for something we could not find, and it was right there, under your nose all along. How many times have you searched around for something and when you went back to the place where you started, there it was. It was there, all along... right in front of you. Try it. Look around the room you are in for something blue. So often we look far away first, then once we find something, we realize that if we just looked down in front of us, there is usually something closer that we could have seen first. I have done this with different groups of people and all have done the same thing. We look farther away first to find what we are looking for. Sometimes, it's not that hard ...

So are you guilty of not seeing what's right in front of you? AND ... more importantly... Are you being seen?

There is a word that I have fallen in love with...Sawubona. It's a Zulu greeting that means "we see you." Orland Bishop, a youth mentor in Los Angeles, explains it best. He says: "Seeing is a dialogue, it establishes you as a witness to a phenomenon. By saying yes, we see each other...It becomes our agreement that seeing has empowered us to investigate our mutual potential for life." Why are we here at THIS exact same time in our lives? You are reading this for a reason. What has this moment given us to be able to accomplish? It's an invitation to participate in each other's lives. This "seeing" of each other also obligates us to give to each other for that moment in each of our lives to be enhanced. How do I have to live and what can I do in order for you to live the life you desire?

Somewhere along the way, we lost the imagination of what sight is and what these inner connections between us really mean. We cannot pursue freedom or success out of self-interest. If we limit one person's freedom and success, then we limit our own. This success is not gained from achieving something but rather it is to be present WITH... And in that presence, we find our inner greatness. Maybe it is time to be seen. Maybe you are hiding too well? Or is there someone around you who needs to be seen?

This "seeing" also reminds me of something I read years ago by the author Robert Fulgham (who wrote the famous book "All I Really Need to Know I Learned in Kindergarten") about the neighborhood game of hide and seek. It was about hiding so well that people cannot find you, about being the one who was always left unfound at the end of the game.

There is hiding, and there is finding. And sometimes, we don't do it right. We don't keep searching until we find... sometimes, we give up right before we find what we are looking for.

And when we hide too well, we get mad at the fact that those who were supposed to be looking didn't find us.

It's funny, isn't it? We often can't see these things in our own lives. It's like hide and seek, grown-up style. But sometimes we just don't take the time to look... to find and to be found.

See, and be seen.

So, Sawubona ...I see you.

Open your eyes...

It is time to be found.

Chapter 49

Believe in Constancy of Purpose.

What is Constancy of Purpose? It is maintaining a focus on your goal and your long-term vision *NO MATTER WHAT.* It's falling and getting back up; it's going around, under or through… it's drive and desire that is unmatched by anything in your life. No Matter What…

And I say NO MATTER WHAT in a way that is non-negotiable.

Gerry Nelson has not had it easy. From a very young age, he has had to overcome many difficult challenges and yet he has persisted through it all and maintained his focus and stayed on track with his vision… See, Gerry wanted to be a pro golfer.

Gerry's story begins at the age of six when he was diagnosed with diabetes. Five years later, he lost his mother to leukemia, and at the age of 23, his father passed away. Losing both parents would have been quite a challenge by itself; however, Gerry's biggest challenge, the one that would completely change his life, would happen two years after his father died. As a result of his diabetes, at the age of 25, Gerry lost his eyesight. He was now blind.

After he lost his sight, Gerry became connected with the United Way and took advantage of the programs that they have to offer the blind. With their help, he went back to school and got a degree in Social Work at Athabasca University. Gerry also started to play golf again, and in 1990, two years after he lost his sight, he began his career as a blind golfer.

Soon after he turned pro, Gerry's golf game took off. He won the Western Canadian Championships five times; he is a two-time winner of the Provincial Championships, and he is also a former Canadian Open champion.

"It's not that we are super men or super women," Gerry states. "We are just like everyone else, looking for a chance to display our potential and our abilities. All we ask is that we be given an opportunity."

That's keeping a focus on the goal, even when you can't physically SEE it ... NO MATTER WHAT.

Life has not been kind to Violet Glaude either. She was born into an abusive home, and when she was older, she entered into an abusive marriage. But Violet was able to break the vicious cycle of abuse when she ended her marriage and moved herself and nine of her 11 children to Edmonton for a fresh start and a new life for all of them.

The family's fresh start was not easy, though. When Violet arrived in Edmonton, she was broke, illiterate, and unable to speak English. Despite these challenges, she was able to find a job and raised her children as a single parent. As her children grew older and finished high school, Violet encouraged them to obtain a post-secondary education. Violet's illiteracy prevented her from helping her children when they encountered academic hardships, but she told her children what she also had to tell herself: "Don't give up, no matter how hard it gets; don't quit."

All of Violet's children followed her mantra, and all of her children were able to finish their post-secondary educations and move on to fulfilling careers.

That is keeping a focus on the long-term vision … NO MATTER WHAT.

And you don't need a personal life struggle to reach deep and believe in that. All you need is an intention that is deep, a desire to be a part of this amazing and intricately complex puzzle of humanity, a desire to make an impact with your life.

With courage and determination, a Saskatoon man named Rocky Bishop personifies this idea in his pursuit to help the less fortunate. A registered nurse, Rocky was motivated by the tragedy that swept through New Orleans as a result of Hurricane Katrina. He was determined to travel to New Orleans to help out in any way he could.

Unfortunately, with many of the phone lines down, Rocky had trouble making contact with anyone in New Orleans. He searched online for contact numbers in phone books, and he talked to anyone he could to find a way to New Orleans.

Some of Rocky's first calls were to search and rescue operations located in Portland, San Diego, and Minnesota. He didn't have any luck getting answers. However, there was light at the end of the tunnel. Rocky made contact with the Department of Home and Health Safety in Washington DC. They gave him a contact number for Lonnie Wascom, the director for emergency services in the North Shore area. Lonnie was receiving dozens of messages every day, but that morning, the first message he listened to was from Rocky. After hearing Rocky's message, Lonnie called and told him to book his flight right away.

Since then, Rocky has been to New Orleans three times. The first time, in November, he went by himself. In January, he took his 15-year-old daughter Melissa. He returned by himself this past June.

This is a story of a man with a goal, a goal to help others in need, a goal to make life better for himself and for those around him. Rocky never quit, and he has forever changed the lives of the people he helped in New Orleans.

These are all stories of Constancy of Purpose. And there are thousands more; each of us has our own. Some days are harder than others, of course. But you have to know what it is you are fighting for before you can even know that you want to fight. SO, …What is your purpose, your desire and passion in life? What gets you out of bed in the morning with the determination to leave a legacy? What is the fire in your gut that makes you go to the end and back of your emotional, physical and mental strength?

Really, what is your purpose?

Find it and don't let it go… NO MATTER WHAT.

Hurry up, the world is waiting for you…

It's time to believe in that again.

Chapter 50

Sit with me in silence...

I drove about three and a half hours to Somerset, Pennnsylvania, tonight, looking at the amazing stars fill the quiet night sky. I am speaking tomorrow at the Pennsylvania State Health and Phys Ed Convention at the Seven Springs Resort. On the ride, tonight's "read" was Dr. Wayne Dyer's CD series about living the life of the Tao. It's called "Change Your Thoughts, Change Your Life." I refer to Dr. Dyer as the man who "saved" my life.

It was October of 2002, and I was in a tough place. I was dealing with a lot of pain in my life, both emotionally and physically. We had just found out the diagnosis that my mom was suffering from this debilitating disease, and my life was just turned upside down by a career change, a move, a breakup, and the physical pain I was dealing with from what the doctors finally discovered was fibromyalgia, a condition which causes a generalized pain that is difficult to trace to its origin. I was also suffering from the loss of my dog, who was my best friend, to illness. I was falling apart. Or so I thought. I allowed myself to think this. I succumbed to the mental, emotional and physical pain. I WAS the pain.

Then, one day, when I was lying in bed, not moving for what seemed like days, I turned on the TV. Flipping through the channels, I stopped on a show where I saw Dr. Dyer speaking to a live audience. I had not really watched or listened to him before. Something didn't let me change the channel. I listened. I heard. I sat up in bed and felt my heart physically molding itself back together while I sat there. I was feeling whole for the first time in months. It felt good. It seemed like Dr. Dyer was speaking directly to ME. I turned off the TV when the show was over, having listened to all two hours of the program. I sat in silence, writing down everything I could remember, writing down my pain, as if writing it on paper would rid my mind of it.

I sat, quietly, and I felt a coolness come over me like a soft breeze on the first fall day after an excruciating summer. I realized in that moment what I thought was the winter of my life was really the spring. It was just an opportunity for me to shed all that didn't serve me, to get rid of that which I didn't deserve. It was my time to let go, to let God decide what was next for me. I was caught up in my own ego, focused on what I didn't have. Instead, It was time to focus on what I did have. "You get that which you manifest." That is one of Dr. Dyer's most famous lines. I have repeated it over and over in my life many times during these past eight years. I have found it to be eerily true. I need reminders. We all do some days.

I was trying to control what wasn't mine to control. I was trying to do instead of be. I was so wrapped up in getting instead of giving. I wasn't following my calling. I didn't even know what my calling was. I was so lost inside my own life. How can that be? I felt like I was supposed to be somewhere, and I could never find where that somewhere was. And since that day, I have been back there a few more times, lost and confused, focused on the wrong things, looking, searching, seeking just to be understood. One of my favorite prayers ever given to the world is the Prayer of St. Francis of Assisi: "Grant that I may not so much seek to be consoled as to console; to be understood as to understand; to be loved as to love. For it is in giving that we receive…"

This is my calling: to give, to understand, to listen, to just …be. I have felt that all my life. I struggle often with living it out. I guess that you may, too.

I listened, smiling as I drove, marveling at the stars through my sunroof. I was trying to live the Tao, and just be; quiet and still. "The breeze at dawn has secrets to tell you. Just be quiet and listen." And even those days when I don't know what my calling is, or I still doubt, after all this time… I have to let go and trust. These words, of course, are the same ones that come out of my mouth to my athletes. Let go, and trust. The knowing is where the miracles happen. If we are just quiet and still, we hear things we may never have heard before in our lives. It's truly amazing…

Let go.

Trust.

Listen.

Sit with me in silence.

Chapter 51

Do It Good. Love, Mom.

I have gotten about 20 or so emails over the past couple of weeks asking where a new blog was… I have been dragging my feet. That is so unlike me when it comes to writing, but it is so like me when it comes to my perfectionism. Here it is. I started this over a week ago, and I kept walking away from it. Tonight, I am going to finish it. I am tired of walking away from what is inside me for fear it won't be good enough. Tonight, I am going to let it be what it is…Real.

So my goal when I started writing these blogs was to write 60. I would then have my goal accomplished to have enough to choose from so I could create a book from what I have written. Since I was a little girl, one of my life's goals has been to publish a book, something in which I could share my thoughts on life with others. I hope that once I can, I will publish it and that I will feel one of my life-long goals in my hands.

I haven't written for over two weeks. I have been waiting … wanting it to be perfect … number 60. I wanted to make it really special. Then I was driving today, and I started thinking about the fact that the more I waited to write it, the less perfect it would become and the more stress I would have to make it so. I have been thinking for months about what the topic of this last one blog should be. What five words could bring it all home? Then I thought about Mom, as always … and I thought about something that she used to say all the time. I found those notes from her that I have saved, the ones she would leave for me in the morning before I left to go to school. They were usually in my cereal bowl she put on the kitchen table for breakfast. She always had a way of reminding me of the little things. But now I know they were the most important things. Like take the garbage out. I look at that now, and I realize how symbolic perhaps that was. Often, it would be followed up with "do it now… if you do, you won't forget." That used to make me laugh. I wouldn't dare forget, or I would hear about it for a long time. But now, I find solace in those words. Taking the garbage out is right where I am in my life. I get it, Mom.

Often her notes were short, but they seem to have such meaning now. It's like watching a children's movie as an adult. It's a new movie. One note said a few different things but included her "do it good" saying and then ended with "Love, Mom." I have carried that with me. It is so simple, but it is something she used to say all the time. "Do it good." No matter what it was, she always wanted to remind me that there was really only one way to do anything.

And it was about whatever I needed to do that day, or today, or on April 13th or on any day I can think of, that was important. I should give with everything I have, and not do things with less. Mom was always good about reminding me of that. I want that to be my motto for my life. Mom was also a grammatist, and she always corrected us when we used the wrong words or parts of speech. But she insisted on using "Do it good" as her way of reminding me that I had a choice of how to expend myself and my energy. There was no point in doing something if I wasn't going to give all of me. I have lived that. And I honor my mother every time I do.

I turned 38 a few days ago, and it was one of the toughest birthdays of my life thus far. I can't really explain why, except that I don't feel like I have done "it" as "good" as I could have. My life story has had as many crescendos and decrescendos as anyone's, and I have certainly created, torn down, started over, and built back up almost every aspect of my life to date, and more than once. My life has been anything but boring.

Birthdays always come around so quickly. I find myself wondering where the year went and what I could have done to maybe stop the passage of time a little bit. I have not yet mastered that feat, and quite honestly, I know I never will. It's a nice pipe dream to have when 40 seems to be just around the corner. Ok, maybe not seems, but IS. The reality of that sinks in deeper as I sit here listening to the crickets making sweet music outside my front door.

"Do it good." I have made a decision as a matter of fact to not allow less from myself. Even though I feel I often give it much by mistake, or by my inability to pull my life together at times, I do what I can with what I have. My choice is to do THAT "good." Regardless. When I screw it all up and I have to start again, I even screw it all up good … At least there was effort involved. I feel like life may never make sense otherwise. I think that's what Mom meant when she said "do it good."

The tenth anniversary of 9/11 was melancholy for us all. That day is a day we will never forget. Like the day the Japanese attacked Pearl Harbor, it is a day that will live in infamy. And those ten years have changed us to the core of who we are and what we find and maybe do not find to be important anymore. Dealing with the aftermath of the tragedy has tested our beliefs and our morals. Who we want to be and the legacy we want to leave are so much more important today than maybe they have ever been. We are a country still mourning, even 10 years later. We are still rebuilding, still asking if we will ever find forgiveness. In that ability to find at some point the forgiveness to heal, I find comfort in knowing that we will never forget. I believe in our ability to heal and to fill in the holes, not with new faces to replace the old, but with new faces to honor and to add value to those who left this earth way too soon, and with no choice of their own.

I spent time last Sunday reading through the names on that list - all of them. A few I knew personally. The youngest was a two-year-old on the flight from Boston. Well over Two thousand people lost their lives that day. The estimated number of children who lost a parent in the tragedy is more than 3,000. I thank God that my nephew wasn't one of them.

The love we give our neighbors, our families, our friends and even those strangers for whom we hold the door heals this country just a little bit faster. I think Mom would be proud that I want to give that love to anyone who crosses my path, honestly and truly. There is no excuse not to do so. And I want to do it "good."

I feel a higher intensity when I yearn to give freely, love abundantly, and feel wholly. I am excited about the possibilities. I am 38 now. I can't stop time. And as I write this tonight, I don't want to. I am not going to worry about it right now. I am not going to worry about if this is worthy of being blog number 60. Sometimes, things are just as they are, and the beauty in that imperfection is its perfection.

Right now, what I have is a full heart, a strong will, and an open mind. And whatever I do with all of that, it will be good. Always.

I have taken out the garbage. I have loved "good."

I have discovered a profound meaning in the little things.

I have learned that in the middle of my deepest pain, or in my hardest fall, I have a voice inside my heart that whispers as loud and as long as I need it to. The good I have learned about on a small torn square piece of scrap paper from January of 1991 will be the good that I will hold forever.

I may have, for the first time 20 years later, fully understood what she meant. I thank you for your patience, Mom.

I got it.

I am doing it good.

Love, Jen.

The End.

"I figured I would find you here."
He smiled at her in a way she had never noticed before.
Maybe she just never really looked.
His warm embrace was more than she could handle.
She stepped back, almost too comfortable too fast.
"I'm supposed to take this slow... "
She said it more to herself than for anyone else to hear, but he responded before she could even finish the sentence.
"You found what you were in search of, don't you get it?"
He was quick in his words, his tone higher pitched than before and a bit rushed.
"No... I guess I don't." She was trying to be honest. Loudly honest... perhaps feeling foolish at actually admitting she had no idea where to go from here.
"So now I am enlightened... So what. I am still staring at the same view as when I started."
He chuckled quietly at her innocence and laughed louder at her inability to realize what she just admitted.
"Yes my love. That's the issue. You are still staring at the same view. Turn around and open your eyes. It's been there all along. You just weren't ready to see it yet."
Happiness, love, awareness of who she is and what she has to give to the world was all right in front of her.

She didn't have to go anywhere.
No searching, no looking, no finding would bring the truth to
her soul.
They already WERE her soul. She just needed to stop looking
long enough to see.
She slowly grabbed Life by the hand and as their fingers
entwined, he melted into her.
She was living all of him now.
Right on time.
And it was good.

"In the still moments of life's true pleasures, I find peace
in knowing happiness.

When my heart and my soul collide, that's where I find
myself. And that, above all else, is what love of life is all
about." --jlc

About the Author

Author Jen Croneberger has been involved in sports since a very young age. She was the CEO/Founder of Excellence Training Camps, Inc. as well as the current president of JLynne Consulting Group, LLC. She has held numerous coaching positions, including the head softball coach at Unionville High School, assistant and head softball coach at Ursinus College and the Mental Game Coach for the (NPF) Women's Professional Softball Team, The Philadelphia Force. She also works with many community groups and organizations on a regular basis including West Chester Communities That Care, Girls Leadership Program, Girls Take Charge Leadership Camp, Girls Leadership Academy and the National icouldbe.org Mentoring Program. Croneberger also spent time as an adjunct professor at Ursinus College, teaching a course on the philosophies and principles of coaching. She has spoken at large conventions including the NFCA National Convention and yearly at the University of Tennessee Softball camp. She was selected by the Chester County Chamber of Business and Industry as the 2009 Female Business Leader of the Year.

Most of Croneberger's last 10 years have been spent working with athletes, instilling confidence and building strength, both mentally and physically. She was consulted by MTV's show "MADE" as a mental skills/fear coach for one of its subjects in the Fall of 2007. Croneberger has also been interviewed on various occasions by Philadelphia's ABC affiliate, Channel 6 Action News, regarding the mental approach of the Philadelphia Phillies before entering into the World Series in 2008 and 2009 as well as the mental approach of the Philadelphia Eagles before entering into the NFL playoffs in 2008. In the Spring of 2010, Channel 6 Action News interviewed Croneberger regarding the mental state of Tiger Woods upon his return to golf.

Croneberger holds her Master's degree from the University of the Rockies in Sports and Performance Psychology. She is also a Member of the Golden Key International Honour Society. She uses everything she has learned and taught over the years to create team-building/team-chemistry seminars as well as keynote speeches for corporate clients, youth leadership programs, women-in-business groups and sports teams of all levels. Mental game coaching seminars and workshops are specifically done for teams (age 11 & up) and coaches for all sports. Confidence, accountability, leadership, getting through adversity, and "playing" for love of the game are some key topics Jen focuses on in all of her presentations.

Croneberger lives in Chester County, PA with her two dogs, Zoe and Apollo.

Croneberger is available for keynotes and seminars by contacting her at www.thefivewords.com

Reviews

"So much of Jen's writing brought back memories of my own childhood... my own interactions with people, that I felt like I was a part of the book as I read it." --Ed White, Freelance Writer, Editor.

"Some excerpts reminded me of the stupidity of walls...life is more beautiful without them. Our souls, hearts, and minds see what we allow them." --Laura Gurenlian Davidson

"A must read for anyone who wants to deepen their awareness and journey into areas they have not yet realized about themselves... I had goosebumps after reading this." --Renee Morgan MSW, LCSW Relationship Therapist

"There comes a time when one is ready to learn...and there is no better way than through story; This is one such story. I have read this 4 times....and I simply love it." --Tom Hurley, Author, Coach

"Jen is one of the most effectively inspirational speakers and writers I've ever come across. Her words reach into your soul like a knife cutting through butter, and you connect immediately. Uplifting, and thought provoking, you'll never feel the same or look at the world in the same light after reading this book."--M. Melissa Blough

"I sat down one evening to read just a chapter. And found myself hours later submersed into Jen's world... Laughing, crying, smiling and thinking 'finally... someone just like me". --Tricia Gardner, TimeSaver VA.